Bead
Crochet

Bethany Barry

INTERWEAVE PRESS
www.interweave.com

Editor: Lorrie LeJeune
Technical Editor: Jean Lampe
Illustrations: Sara Boore, Marjorie C. Leggitt
Photography: Joe Coca
Photo styling: Ann Swanson
Cover and interior design: Karen Schober
Production: Dean Howes and Samantha L. Thaler
Copyeditor: Stephen Beal
Proofreader and Indexer: Nancy Arndt

 Interweave Press, Inc.
201 East Fourth Street
Loveland, Colorado 80537-5655 USA
www.interweave.com

Printed in Singapore by Imago

Library of Congress Cataloging-in-Publication Data

Barry, Bethany, 1953-
  Bead crochet : a beadwork how-to / Bethany Barry.
     p. cm.
Includes index.
  ISBN 1-931499-42-X
  1. Beadwork. 2. Crocheting. I. Title.
  TT860.B3335 2004
  745.58'2--dc22

                                2003023190

10 9 8 7 6 5 4 3

Contents

Introduction to Bead Crochet

WHY WRITE A BOOK ON BEAD CROCHET? Because beading is an exploding field of colorful creativity, and bead crochet offers unique and exciting ways to use and play with beads. This book will get you started on the path.

My journey into bead crochet began after several years of learning, using, and teaching the conventional seed-bead stitches. Peyote, brick, and Ndebele stitches were fine, but, like a bored heroine trapped in a terrible novel, I secretly longed for more. At *Stitches*, a wonderful fiber arts show, I saw irresistible fibers in a multitude of brilliant colors and textures. I succumbed to the temptation and bought many, despite having no idea how to use them. I knew how to do simple single crochet, so I made myself a purse, using four or five different colors and types of yarn, including eyelash, and embellished it with beads. I used that purse constantly, and received many compliments and questions about its origin and design.

Several years ago, I took a class to learn how to make a bead crochet rope. Using a combination of ideas and techniques, I began experimenting with different forms of bead crochet, and fell in love with it. Crochet is an extremely forgiving stitch, and unlike traditional seed-bead stitchery, crochet mistakes are easy to pull out and redo, or to hide. The possibilities of bead crochet are endless, and I hope that you, too, will become hooked on this technique (pun absolutely intended: the French word *crochet* means "hook").

Emma Post Barbour, who wrote *The New Bead Book* in 1924, said: " . . . we wish to leave you with this thought—that beadwork is always worthwhile; though fashion may change there is always a return to the beaded; the artistic work of your hands today will give you much satisfaction while the vogue is strong, and a work of art always lives, becoming much enhanced by age in both value and sentiment." This statement is as accurate now as it was then, and I hope that you will keep it in mind as you advance along your own beading journey.

History of Bead Crochet

THE NEEDLE ARTS HAVE BEEN IN EXISTENCE FOR A LONG TIME. We know of garments found in ancient Egyptian tombs with a form of primitive edging that is reminiscent of lace. Crochet and lace are closely related, so theoretically this stitching could have been an early form of crochet lace. Sadly, due to the fragility of fiber, we can do little more than guess at when crochet began as few ancient samples remain.

In his *Sacred History of Knitting*, Heinz Edgar Kiewe traces knitting needles and crochet hooks back to the beginnings of Christianity. Concluding that crochet hooks were likely everyday implements of the time, he refers to a story about Akida ben Joseph (A.D. 50–137), a follower of Christ, who was said to have crocheted with a hook so he might spend his time as a shepherd more usefully. It follows that the art of crochet was first practiced by shepherds who retrieved the sheep's wool they found snagged on bushes in the fields. They spun the wool and made warm garments for themselves using a carefully carved stick with a curved end. These crude sticks evolved into the bone or ivory hooks that were used by sixteenth-century Irish nuns to make exquisite crocheted lace.

Various schools of needlework, crochet, and lacework appeared in England around the same time. These schools, founded and sponsored by princesses and members of the royal household, sold their needlework, crocheting, and lacework to the public whenever possible. In Europe, a close association existed between needlework and the convent. Fine lace was much valued, and from the thirteenth to the sixteenth centuries, lacemaking was the work of nuns in much the same way that the illumination of manuscripts was the work of monks; it was a form of dedication of work and service to God. Written evidence implies that point lace, bobbin lace, and other forms of needlework were considered more legitimate than crochet at that time, but by the seventeenth century, crochet was again a popular form of convent needlework.

In the nineteenth century, needlework became fashionable as the middle class sought to emulate the upper classes and royalty. In Ireland, during the Potato Famine of the mid-1800s, more than a million died through starvation and poverty. The ability to crochet allowed many people to survive this difficult time. Crocheted handwork generated income, and promoted self respect. An energetic early feminist named Mrs. W. C. Roberts, of County Kildare, started a cooperative needlework arts training school for all family members (including the men). She saw the demand for knitwear in her country declining due to the Industrial Revolution, and as an experiment, she changed from knitting to crochet. It was an immeasurable success, both among families and as a commercial product. As a requirement of teaching someone to crochet, Mrs. Roberts insisted that that person teach thirty other people. This early example of the pyramid scheme (minus the financial angle) insured that crochet would become popular and well known.

The Irish who immigrated to the United States

Vintage bead crochet purses. Courtesy of Carol Perrenoud.

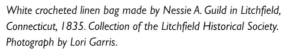

White crocheted linen bag made by Nessie A. Guild in Litchfield, Connecticut, 1835. Collection of the Litchfield Historical Society. Photograph by Lori Garris.

brought their crochet skills with them, and as a result, by 1863, many patterns for crochet had been published, and special crochet threads and fibers had become available. Filet crochet, later known as square-stitched crochet, became the most popular form of crochet. It was always done in pure white cotton to define holiness and to symbolize purity. Doilies and antimacassars are enduring examples of this delicate Victorian art, which combined decorative as well as utilitarian qualities.

In Victorian times, beadwork was considered ornamental rather than practical. It required leisure time, a certain level of financial stability, interest in the art, and manual dexterity. As early as the 1820s, many women's academies included beadwork in their curricula. At Miss Pierce's Academy in Litchfield, Connecticut, students were taught bead crochet and bead knitting to make bags, miser's purses, reticules, and tubular purse handles.

Purchasing goods with currency, as opposed to barter, was becoming common by the mid- to late-1700s. As a result, the average person needed a way to carry money and have easy access to it. The miser's purse, also called a long purse, ring purse, or

Beaded bag made by Mabel Strong Seymour at Miss Pierce's Academy, c. 1830. Silk, polychrome glass beads. Collection of the Litchfield Historical Society. Photograph by Lori Garris.

Stuffed bead crochet bracelet with a hook to hold a ball of yarn. Courtesy of Carol Perrenoud.

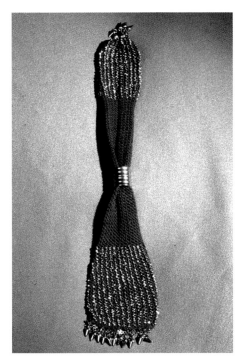

Red miser's bag crocheted. Maker unknown, silk and metal beads, c. 1830. Collection of the Litchfield Historical Society. Photograph by Lori Garris.

Green miser's purse from the late 1800s. Courtesy of Carol Perrenoud.

stocking purse, appeared in the 1780s, and was the first portable money container used by both men and women. These ingenious small bags were shaped like a figure eight, with a slit in the middle for insertion of the money. The purse had two movable rings of steel, silver, or gold, which prevented the loss of coins through the slit, and were often looped over a belt. Miser's purses could be beaded, knitted, crocheted or stitched; some were embellished with beaded tassels; they were another example of decorative and functional design.

By the 1920s, bead crochet was used to create necklace ropes and bracelets, as well as beaded bags. These items were the perfect accessories to the playful, jazzy, beaded dresses that Flappers were wearing. Many women made their own purses since beads and supplies were plentiful, and a wealth of patterns were advertised in newspapers and magazines. These advertisements were placed by the suppliers and manufacturers of silk-twist threads and yarns, beads, purse frames, and other necessary components for the designs. Brainerd & Armstrong, in New London, Connecticut,

Miser's purse. Courtesy of Carol Perrenoud.

promoted "purse-making as a convenient and practical way to become a home artisan," and the company became a leader in published embroidery lessons and instructions for knitting and crocheting silk bags and purses, both with and without beads. The beads for these purses were imported from Europe, sold in bunches of twelve strings, and numbered according to size. Many of the vintage bead-crochet instructions involved stringing beads, crocheting a row, then breaking the thread and starting another row. This tedious process was repeated for each row! Luckily, we have since developed bead-crochet techniques that are less time-consuming.

The popularity of crochet is cyclical, as is the case with most needlework. Interest in bead crochet and beaded bags died out in the early 1930s, along with other forms of handwork, such as bead knitting and embroidery. The Depression, the changing roles of women, availability of inexpensive manufactured goods, World War II, and

Victorian bag in dark blue cotton and steel beads c. mid-1800s. Courtesy of Doris Coghill.

Turkish snake. Courtesy of Carol Perrenoud.

the loss of "free time" all played a part in the decline of crochet, and especially bead crochet.

Crochet has seen a significant revival in the past twenty years through the innovative work of Sylvia Cosh, James Walters, and others. Interest in bead crochet was somewhat limited until Carol Perrenoud and Lydia Borin arose to lead the bead-crochet revival, and they've been joined by many other creative women who have been testing the waters of bead crochet, and who are opening the floodgates of bead crochet possibilities. This book is your chance to jump in and join us!

Beaded bag with fringe. Maker unknown, polychrome glass beads and silk, c. 1835. Collection of the Litchfield Historical Society. Photograph by Lori Garris.

Beaded bag, owned by Mrs. Francis Bacon of Litchfield, Connecticut, 1845. Polychrome glass beads and silk. Collection of the Litchfield Historical Society. Photograph by Lori Garris.

A collection of vintage and contemporary silver, bone, wood, and steel crochet hooks.

Materials and Notions for Bead Crochet

THE MOST IMPORTANT TOOL FOR BEAD CROCHET is the crochet hook and it is supported by materials such as threads, yarns, and beads. You'll find crochet hooks in a wide range of sizes, made of wood, plastic, steel, and aluminum. The material the hook is made from is largely irrelevant; use the hook that feels best for you and in the proper size for the work you're doing.

U.S. and European sizes for hooks are different, and only recently have manufacturers attempted to standardize them in metric sizes. The type of fiber or stitch size you choose for a project determines the hook size. Most hooks can be purchased at fabric and yarn stores, as well as craft supply stores.

Hooks

When you're choosing a hook, it's important to select a size that feels comfortable in your hand and allows you to work without distraction. Here are some observations I've made about crochet hooks:

- Aluminum hooks are very light, and come in lettered sizes, with "A" the smallest and "K" the largest. I use aluminum hooks for crocheting with multiple strands.

▦ Plastic hooks tend to be weaker and more brittle than hooks made of other materials. They are also harder to work with because they sometimes stick as you push them through stitches.

▦ Steel hooks are made in numbered sizes: the higher the number, the smaller the hook. In general, steel hooks are used for fine work, such as making lace or doilies, but they're also great for bead crochet. Steel hooks are sometimes labeled with both European and American sizes. The Boye size 0 steel hook is my favorite for working with Mastex thread and beads.

▦ Wooden hooks are usually hand-carved from exotic hardwoods such as rosewood or walnut. They often have beautiful, intricately turned shafts and are light and easy to work with.

Threads and Yarns

Many types of threads and yarns (referred to as fiber from hereafter) may be used for bead crochet. The determining factors for your choice are usually the thickness of the fiber and the size of the holes in the beads. If you're using size 11 seed beads, you will need to use a fine fiber. If you're using size 5 seed beads, trade beads, polymer clay beads, or other beads with large holes, your fiber can be heavier and thicker. You can use a wide range of fiber including wool, cotton, waxed linen, nylon, and polyester, as well as designer yarns, ribbons, rope, or other media. Beading threads such as Nymo D and F, Silamide, or C-Lon work very well with size 11 or smaller seed beads. Nymo F is the heaviest and thickest of the Nymo threads. It's available only in black or white, and I use black almost exclusively when I'm stringing beads, regardless of their color. Although I list this thread with the crochet threads, I rarely use Nymo F to crochet, only to string beads.

*Examples of fibers including
Mastex, waxed and bonded
polyester, and Gudebrod silk*

Remember, it is important to really like the fiber you're using. It should feel good to the touch, and you should enjoy looking at it. It's also important to recognize that your fiber may have the potential for skin irritations and/or allergic reactions in the wearer.

My favorite fiber for bead crochet is Mastex, a strong, twisted nylon upholstery thread with a soft sheen. Mastex is available only in muted colors, so I also use bonded or waxed polyester when I want bright shades of purple, green, red, and blue.

Designer yarns

Beads

Beads come in a breathtaking assortment of sizes, shapes, and colors, and you can use many of them in bead crochet. Seed beads in sizes 8°, 5°, and 6° generally work best with Mastex, and their large hole sizes make them easy to string. Japanese seed beads tend to be regular in size and color. Czech seed beads are irregular, and while they are attractive, their variable hole sizes can cause problems for stringing. Small accent beads such as magatamas, triangles in sizes 5 and 8, squares, teardrops, daggers, and M&Ms (glass, not chocolate) can be used successfully. Miracle beads, fiber-optic beads, or other 4–8mm glass beads, ovals, diamond-shapes, leaves, hearts, and flowers, work well, too. You can use just about any bead as long as the fiber will fit through its hole.

Bead crochet uses a lot of fiber, and it's hard to gauge how much you'll need, so it's best to work from the spool whenever you can. When you're stringing beads, **do not cut the fiber from the spool**. Instead, string your beads and wind everything back on the spool. If you run out of beads, you can always add more, but don't cut the fiber. (See Crochet Techniques section.)

Beads and supplies

Miscellaneous Supplies

▦ Big Eye needles are among my favorite needles for stringing. They come in two lengths: 2" or 5" (6.5 or 12.5 cm). Experience and personal preference will determine the size you choose. Stringing the beads can take time, and Big Eye needles will speed up the process.

- Beading needles: I use these needles for embellishment, fringes, or accents, and I prefer the English steel needles in sizes 10 or 12.

Bead spinner and a spool of Mastex

- Bead spinners are useful, but not essential, for bead stringing. You can use a special curved needle with a bead spinner to quickly scoop up the beads as they spin around. Bead spinners come in many forms. They can be handmade of beautiful (and expensive) polished hardwoods, or constructed on a simpler scale from less expensive materials.

- Scissors: I use a pair of sharp embroidery scissors.

- Paper clips or safety pins mark where you stop working. Stitch markers are useful for marking the beginning of each spiral round, and they won't snag the fiber.

- Mandrels are spindles used to hold a tubular piece of beaded single crochet while you work, or store crochet beads until you're ready to use them. A mandrel keeps the tube center open, which is important when making crochet beads, and will help prevent beaded single crochet ropes and tubes from becoming distorted, because it's easy to see the stitches as you work around the spindle, and not miss any. I use wooden skewers (for shish kebab) from the grocery store. Skewers are inexpensive and come in two diameters, which you can cut to a shorter length if needed. Wooden or bamboo knitting needles will also serve as a mandrel.

- Beading surfaces can be anything that keeps your beads from rolling or bouncing. Vellux is one of my favorites, but you can also use chamois, flannel, velvet, or a towel.

- Light is critical. Your work area should be well lit. Use specialty lights to focus on the project. Ott lights are excellent, as are goose-necked or swing-arm lamps.

▦ Nail polish or glue seals knots (and stiffens fiber, as described below). You can use a butane or disposable lighter to melt nylon threads. However, be extremely cautious, lest you set your piece on fire or burn yourself.

▦ Nail polish or correction fluid, such as Liquid Paper, Wite-Out, or other brands stiffens thread so it may be used as a needle. Use about 1–1½" (2.5–3.8 cm) on the tip of the thread to stiffen for use as a needle. An added plus when using this method, the white tip will make it easy to see when stringing beads.

▦ Beeswax coats thread. I prefer it to anything else, because its weight strengthens and smooths the thread while reducing tangles. Use beeswax lavishly to coat Nymo thread when you're working with a double strand: thread the needle, fold the thread in half, and pull both strands through the wax at the same time to join them as one.

▦ A pair of fine chain-nosed pliers are an invaluable tool for bead crochet. Pliers will help you pull a stubborn thread through your work or break an extra or incorrect bead.

Assortment of beading notions

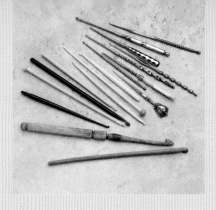

Crochet Tips and Techniques

The crochet techniques in this chapter cover the basic methods I use to make the designs in the book. They're not meant to replace a good learn-to-crochet book. For readers who want more information about crochet, I recommend *The Crocheter's Companion* by Nancy Brown (Interweave Press, 2002).

Getting Started

HOLDING THE HOOK

People hold their hooks in two ways: as a pencil, or as a knife. Practice both methods and decide which one is most comfortable for you.

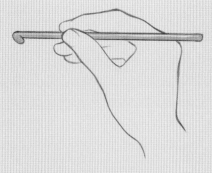

Holding the hook as a pencil

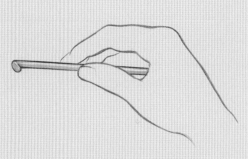

Holding the hook as a knife

HOLDING THE YARN

Hold the yarn in the hand opposite the one holding the hook. If you're right-handed, hold the yarn in your left hand, over the index finger, and under the middle finger. From here, you may find it comfortable to allow the yarn to strand over your ring finger and under your little finger, or to strand over your index finger, under your middle finger, and then hang down inside your palm with your ring and little fingers lightly closed. Practice both methods and decide which feels comfortable for you. When you begin to crochet, stabilize the work by holding the yarn tail that trails from the slipknot between your left middle finger and left thumb. After working a few rows, hold the work with your left middle finger and left thumb slightly below the hook. Reverse these positions if you're left-handed.

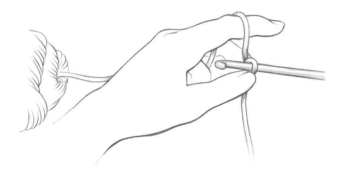

Holding the yarn in the left hand

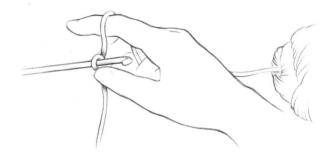

Holding the yarn in the right hand

Slipknot

Crochet usually begins with a slipknot. Make a circle of yarn about 4–6" (10–15 cm) from the tail end. Pull the working yarn through the center of the circle with your hook to make a loop. This loop remains on the hook. Pull on the yarn tail to straighten, and then pull on the working yarn to adjust the size of the loop to fit your hook.

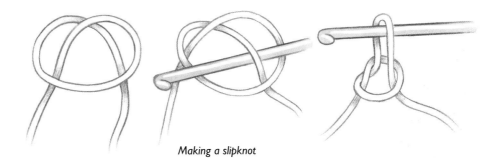

Making a slipknot

YARNOVER (YO)

Making a yarnover

An important step in crochet, the yarnover is worked with each stitch at least once. With the hook pointing down through the first stitch, hold the hook and stitch in place with your right hand, then wrap the working yarn from behind and over the hook toward you. The hook should be facing you, to catch the yarn. Always bring the working yarn over the hook from back to front when you're making the yarnover.

The Crochet Chain

BASE CHAIN (CH)

Making a base chain

The base chain, or foundation row, starts with a slipknot. Place the knot on the hook, then work a yarnover and pull the yarn through the loop on the hook to create the first chain stitch. *Yo the hook, pull yarn through the loop on the hook to make another chain; repeat from *, making chains until you have the desired number or length required. Practice the base chain until the tension and stitches are even. The base chain is usually worked without beads.

COUNTING CHAINS

The loop on the hook is never included in the stitch count. To count chains, begin with the first chain below the hook, then count each chain to the end, or vice versa (count the chain at the very end as the first chain, and work upward with the chain below the hook counted as the last). The slipknot isn't counted as a stitch in either direction.

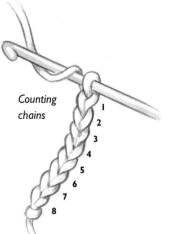

Counting chains

Crochet Stitches for bead crochet

SINGLE CROCHET (SC)

This is the main stitch used in bead crochet, and is the most commonly used crochet stitch.

To make the stitch (these instructions apply to either hand): Insert the hook from front to back through the base chain or single crochet, yarnover, and draw up a loop with the hook facing you. You now have 2 loops on your hook, yarnover, and draw hook through both loops, one loop remains on hook. You've now completed one single crochet.

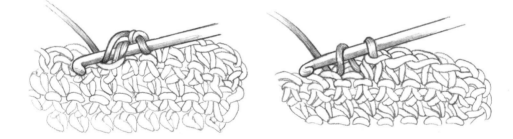

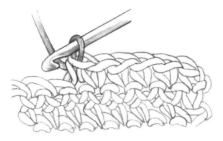

SLIP STITCH (SL ST)

This stitch is commonly used to join other stitches. Insert the hook into the next stitch, yarnover, and in one motion draw the loop through the chain (or stitch) and the loop on the hook. The slip stitch adds no height to the work, and is used to move the yarn across the stitches without adding height. In bead crochet, the slip stitch is another form of working (see Beading Techniques, page 29). Slip stitch is not used exclusively to crochet, it can be applied to knitting and woven fabric. It also makes a good cord when used after making a chain in the desired size. To make the cord, crochet a chain to desired length, then work a slip stitch in each chain.

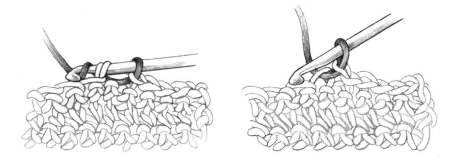

TURNING CHAINS (TC) FLAT

Turning chains are used in flat crochet, and in some methods of circular crochet, to bring the work up to the height needed to make the next stitch. Whether to make the turning chain at the end of the row or the beginning varies with crocheters and crochet books. Some crocheters work the chain at the end of the row, while others turn their work first and begin the new row with a chain. Either method is acceptable, but it's important to be consistent within each piece, otherwise your stitch numbers will not remain constant. In single crochet, the standard to use is one chain. A single chain is the same height as a single crochet stitch. However, in my flat bead crochet work, I frequently use two chains to turn single crochet instead of the standard, because it keeps the width of the piece consistent.

Turning chains

A slip stitch doesn't need a turning chain, because it adds no height to the work.

Changing the shape
INCREASING AND DECREASING

If the length or circumference of the chain is smaller than required, you will need to add stitches. To do this, simply work two single crochet in one stitch as many times as needed.

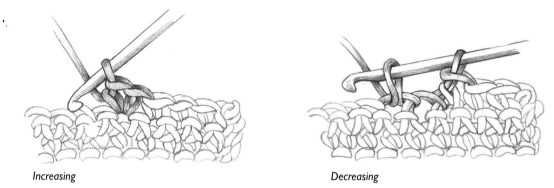

Increasing   *Decreasing*

If your work is too large, you'll need to subtract stitches or decrease by one of several methods. If the gap won't show in your work, or distort the appearance of the finished item, simply skip a stitch, work the next st, skip again if needed, single crochet, and continue. If the piece requires a smooth appearance, work the decrease over two single crochet as follows: Insert the hook into the next sc, work a yo and pull up a loop (2 loops on hook). Insert the hook into the next sc, yo and pull up a loop (3 loops on hook), yo and pull through all three loops. This counts as one decrease. Repeat as necessary.

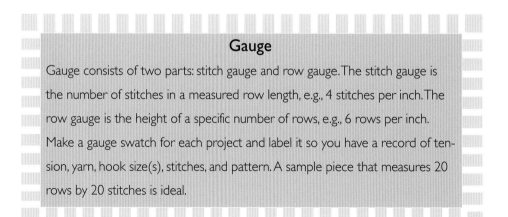

Gauge

Gauge consists of two parts: stitch gauge and row gauge. The stitch gauge is the number of stitches in a measured row length, e.g., 4 stitches per inch. The row gauge is the height of a specific number of rows, e.g., 6 rows per inch. Make a gauge swatch for each project and label it so you have a record of tension, yarn, hook size(s), stitches, and pattern. A sample piece that measures 20 rows by 20 stitches is ideal.

Adding new yarns when working flat

When adding new colors or yarns, try to attach the new yarn at the end of the row or round by joining within the last stitch. Doing so will make it easier to weave the tails into a seam. When the design requires joining a new yarn within the row, work up to the last step in the stitch with the old yarn (before the final yarnover), then work the final yarnover with the new yarn and draw through all loops. Continue working with the new yarn. Leave about 4" (10 cm) of tail from both yarns to weave in later.

TYING IN

You can also join yarns by simply tying the end of the new yarn into a stitch on the row below, then drop the old yarn and begin crocheting with the new one. To secure the ends when you're using this method, cut the old yarn and place the tails from both old and new yarns across the tops of the next few stitches and work over the ends. If crocheting over the extra yarn results in bulky stitches or is visible in your work, tie the yarn on as previously directed, then cut the old yarn leaving a 4" (10 cm) tail. After the work is finished, weave one tail in along the wrong side of the stitches in one direction and the other tail in the opposite direction.

Flat crochet, worked back and forth

This technique is worked in rows, not rounds. One row of single crochet is the right side of the work, one row the wrong side. Either row can be used as the right side, so decide which one is the right side of the work and mark with a safety pin.

The following instructions make a sample of flat, back-and-forth single crochet using 1 or 2 chains for turning (I use 2 chains).

Foundation row: Chain the number of stitches as specified in the instructions, then chain 2 more to act as the turning chain. Turn the piece so you're always working from right to left if you're right-handed, top to bottom, and from left to right if you're left-handed.

Row 1: Insert the hook in the third ch from the hook (to prevent the piece from increasing or decreasing). Work sc in each chain across row. Ch 2, turn work.

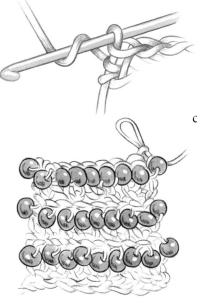

Flat bead crochet

Row 2: Insert hook into second sc from side edge, work sc in each st of previous row. Ch 2, turn work.

Repeat Row 2 (or follow specific design instructions).

When bead crochet is worked flat, in rows, the beads are inserted every other row, on the right side of the work. Note that the beads appear on every other row.

Circular flat crochet

Working single crochet

This method is worked in rounds and is the flat technique originally used for doilies, antimacassars (pieces made to protect chair and sofa backs from the oil of Macassar used by Victorian men for their hair), and other decorative pieces.

There are three methods of working circular flat crochet.

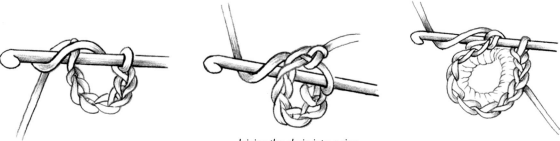

Joining the chain into a ring

CONTINUOUS ROUNDS, WITHOUT JOINS OR TURNS:

This method is used primarily in single crochet, and the rounds are worked in a spiral fashion without joining or turning.

ROUNDS WITHOUT TURNS:

In this method, each round is joined with a slip stitch at the top of the beginning chain, work a chain for height, but don't turn the work. Single crochet to the end of the round and join with a slip stitch. Unlike the spiral method mentioned previously, these rounds have a definite, visible joining line that cannot be avoided. The joining line curves toward the right or left depending whether the crocheter is left- or right-handed.

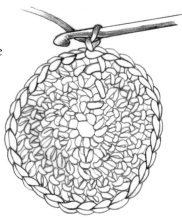

ROUNDS WITH TURNS:

Each round is joined with a slip stitch at the top of the beginning chain, or the first stitch in each subsequent round, and the work is turned at the beginning of the next round. This method also has a visible joining line that remains straight and does not curve to the left or the right.

Here are two examples of working single crochet in flat circular rounds.

METHOD 1:

Continuous spirals of single crochet.

Chain the given number of stitches, join the ch into a circle with sl st.

Round 1: Insert hook into the center of the circle and work a specified number of single crochet sts, usually double the number of chains in the foundation row. Crocheters usually find this method easy to get started. Another technique requires inserting the hook into each ch to work single crochet sts.

Rnd 2 and subsequent rnds: Continue working sc in each st, and increasing as necessary to maintain flat, even edges. The final rnd finishes with a slip st.

METHOD 2: ROUNDS WITHOUT TURNING.

This is only one example of this technique, and instructions for this method can vary from pattern to pattern. Some crocheters may count the turning ch as a stitch after the foundation row, and others may not, so always follow the specific pattern instructions.

Chain the specified number of stitches given in the instructions, join ch into a circle with sl st.

Round 1: Ch 1 for height and count as first stitch. Work 2 sc in each foundation ch, or work a given number of sts into the center of the circle, then sl st to join.

Round 2: Ch 1 for height, and count as first st. Work 2 sc in each st to end of rnd, join rnd with sl st.

Round 3: Ch 1 for height, and count as first st. *Work 2 sc in next st, then 1 sc in next st*; repeat instructions between * * to end of rnd, and join rnd with sl st.

Round 4: Ch 1 for height, count as first st. *Work 2 sc in next st, then 1 sc in each of next 2 st*; repeat instructions between * * to end of rnd, join rnd with sl st.

Round 5: Ch 1 for height, count as first st. *Work 2 sc in next st, then 1 sc in each of next 3 sts*; repeat instructions between * * to end of rnd, join rnd with sl st.

Round 6: Ch 1 for height, count as first st. *Work 2 sc in next sc, then 1 sc in each of next 4 sc*; repeat instructions between * * to end of rnd, join rnd with sl st.

Continue in this pattern until the piece is the desired size. Keep stretching and flattening the work so the edges don't curl up. (If you'd prefer a miniature hat, however, go ahead and let it curl.)

Tubular crochet

This method is circular, but not flat, and forms a tube. I begin my tubular crochet in the same manner as flat circular crochet; work the desired number of chains then join into a circle with a slip stitch. The number of stitches varies according to the desired diameter; my designs normally use a chain of 6. The number of foundation chains is important to remember when you're working with a pattern, because the threading sequence varies according to the number of stitches in the circle. If you are right-handed, you will always be working counterclockwise around the chain. If you are left-handed, you will always be working clockwise. After joining the chain, and working a round or two, the tube is then placed on a mandrel (see Materials and Notions, page 11) to ensure that you're working upward in rounds and forming a tube, and not outward, as in flat circular crochet. When you're working the tubular crochet designs in this book, increases aren't necessary.

Tubular crochet in a spiral pattern

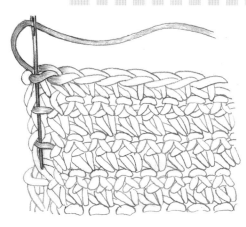

Tubular crochet on a mandrel

The number of chains and rounds worked will determine the desired size of the piece. One of the joys of tubular crochet is that you can continue working your way around the tube adding beads continually, unlike flat, back and forth crochet where you add beads on alternate rows only.

When your tubular piece is resting on the mandrel, the mandrel will be between you and the crochet hook. The mandrel helps maintain even tension in the work, a consistent number of stitches, *and* an even center hole. Without a mandrel, it's very easy for a tube to become distorted, shrink, expand, or lose beads. The mandrel is the key to successful, easy, even bead crochet tubes or ropes. The first design in the book, Spiral Earrings, includes an illustration of work on a mandrel, see page 42.

Measurement for Tubular Bead Crochet

My patterns use 6 beads around, which is a common diameter. Using 8° seed beads, you will need to string 5" (12.5 cm) to get 1" (2.5 cm) of tubular bead crochet. Using 6° seed beads, you will need to string 5½" (14 cm) of beads for 1" (2.5 cm). Using 11° seed beads, you need to string 6" (15 cm).

Finishing/weaving in ends

Always cut the thread leaving a long tail to crochet over, or weave in through the wrong side of the work. I usually leave 4–6" (10–15 cm). For slippery fibers like silk, leave a longer tail. Use a yarn needle or a crochet hook to weave the tails through the stitches or along the side edges of rows, then use a dab of clear nail polish to secure the last little bit of woven-in thread.

Posture and hand movements

Sit in a comfortable straight-backed chair with adequate back support. Position your elbows at waist or hip height and work over your lap or a table surface. Resting your elbows on the table will strain your neck and shoulders. Keep your hands relaxed, and hold the hook lightly, but firmly. Take breaks to roll your shoulders around, stretch your neck, and turn your head from side to side. Be sure to put the hook down to stretch your fingers and relax your arms and hands.

My favorite seat has no back at all; it's a backless meditation/computer chair that you kneel on. I find that it completely eliminates any back or neck strain for me, and I can bead or crochet for hours without tiring.

Tension

This extremely important aspect of bead crochet determines the number of stitches and beads needed for your designs. Some crocheters hold their hooks in a death grip, creating very tight, very small stitches through which it's nearly impossible to insert the hook. Crocheters who are too relaxed make big, loose stitches. Aim for the middle path and you'll always be satisfied with your work.

Beading Tips and Techniques

THERE ARE MANY DIFFERENT BEADING TECHNIQUES, and lots of good books about them. *Creative Bead Weaving* by Carol Wilcox Wells (Sterling,1998), is excellent, as is *The Beader's Companion* by Judith Durant and Jean Campbell (Interweave Press, 1998). In this chapter, I discuss the beading techniques used in this book rather than beading techniques in general. I have combined off-loom beadweaving techniques with bead crochet in some of the projects in this book, and with permission from Interweave Press, I have included diagrams and instructions from *The Beader's Companion* for peyote, square, brick, and ladder stitches, and Ndebele (herringbone weave).

Stringing the beads
Beads are strung onto a **spool of thread**, using a bead spinner, a Big Eye needle, or by hand.

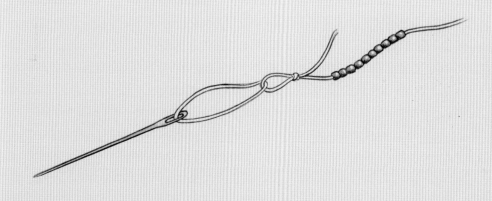

To use the bead spinner—Pour the beads into the spinner bowl. Thread a bead spinner needle, which is long and curved at one end, with one end of a spool of thread. Place the spinner needle sideways across the beads in the back of the spinner bowl, with the curved point facing away from you. Turn the bead spinner counter-clockwise, and watch the beads start collecting on the needle end. It can take a bit of practice to get started with a bead spinner, but it's a great tool for quickly stringing a random assortment, bead soup, or beads of all one color.

Big Eye needle—This specialty needle is almost all eye, and is very easy to thread. It works especially well when using thicker thread, such as Mastex, with 8°s or 6°s. Big Eye needles are fragile, and break easily so it's good to have several on hand.

Make a needle from the thread—A very handy technique that's especially useful when making a design that requires the thread to pass through the beads several times. A stiffened thread end will usually pass through beads easily—sometimes more easily than a needle. Cut the thread end at an angle, and then dip 1"–1½"(2.5–3.8 cm) into a bottle of white correction fluid, or bright-colored nail polish. Let it dry completely, dip the end again, and let it dry until stiff. The white or colored end also makes the thread easier to see when stringing smaller beads.

Running out of beads

If you run out of beads while crocheting, cut off the thread, and pull it through the last loop to keep your work from unraveling. String more beads onto a new thread, tie it in, as if joining a new yarn (see Crochet Techniques, page 17), and continue crocheting. Weave or stitch both loose thread ends to the wrong side and through several stitches or beads to secure. Clip the tail close to the work.

Framing

I use "framing" as a basic pattern of stringing the beads and crocheting with them. String the beads in groups of 3: a small bead, a larger bead, and then a small bead. The two smaller beads frame the larger bead. When you sc with beads in that grouping style, they hang as little clusters, and are quite attractive. For example: string an 8° seed bead, then a 4mm round, and another 8° seed bead. Framing can also be interspersed with groups of other beads.

Framing

Stitches

Slip stitch and single crochet (see Crochet Techniques, page 17) are the two forms of bead crochet I use in this book.

Slip-stitch bead crochet—This method is worked as a tube, and I use at least one bead in every stitch. Begin with a chain, join it into a circle, and then work in rounds. When you look at slip-stitch bead crochet, note that the bead holes are oriented in a north-south position, with the thread traveling vertically up and down.

Single-crochet bead crochet—I prefer single-crochet bead crochet, and use it in most of my designs. I usually work with multiple beads, and use a variety of bead styles and sizes. In this method, the bead holes are oriented in an east-west position, with the thread passing through the bead horizontally. As noted in Crochet Techniques, page 17, this method can be worked in various shapes using flat, tubular, or flat circular methods.

Slip-stitch crochet tube

Single crochet, thread side

Single crochet, beaded side

Flat bead crochet can be a little tricky when starting out, but be patient, and it will get easier as you become familiar with both the tension and the number of beads you need. I usually work with 3–6 beads at a time, and I'll have 3–4" (7.5–10 cm) of beads strung and positioned near the hook. Slide 3 (or specified number) beads up to the front next to the hook, and hold behind the hook, out of the way, work 1 sc with beads, slide 3 more beads to the front, holding them behind the hook, work another sc, slide another 3 beads, and so on, repeating the process to the end of the row, work the turning chain, and then sc the next row without beads.

Note: When you're working flat bead crochet, always alternate rows with and without beads, because the beads automatically fall to the back of the work on wrong side rows. If you forget and include beads on two or more consecutive rows, it will quickly become apparent. Pull out those rows and begin again. Stop at the beginning of each row and check your work to ensure that the stitches and tension are even, and that you're getting the desired look.

Measurements for flat bead crochet—15" (38 cm) of strung beads will equal about 1½" (3.8 cm) of flat bead crochet, using 2–3 beads at a time. This ratio applies to all size beads–*see specific projects for exact lengths.*

Mistakes

You can fix mistakes by adding or dropping stitches, hiding them with more stitches or beads, or by removing the incorrect crochet stitches. If you have too many beads in one place, take a pair of pliers and break the offending beads to remove them. Free-form crochet allows you to stitch over the space, embellish on top of it, or just keep beading. If you have to take a section apart, crochet is remarkably easy to pull out and redo.

Off-Loom stitches

Some of the following terms and illustrations are excerpted from *The Beader's Companion* (Interweave Press, 1998).

Flat peyote stitch—This stitch is often called "one-drop" or "single–drop" when worked one bead at a time. This generic peyote stitch, somewhat different from the Native American-style peyote stitch, will be sufficient for most published patterns.

Even-count flat peyote—Begin by stringing an even number of beads, twice the number you want in one row. These beads will become the first and second rows. Create the next row by stringing one bead and passing through the second-to-last bead of the previous row. String another bead and pass through the fourth-to-last bead of the previous row. Continue adding one bead at a time, passing over every other bead of the previous row.

Two-drop peyote stitch—The two-drop (also called "double-drop") is worked the same as flat peyote, but with two beads at a time instead of one. Begin by stringing an even number of beads. Create the next row by stringing two beads and passing through the third-and fourth-to-last beads of the previous row. String two more beads and pass through the seventh-and eighth-to-last beads of the previous row. Continue adding two beads at a time, passing over every other pair of beads in the previous row.

Tubular peyote stitch—Begin by determining the diameter of the form you wish to cover. Leaving at least a 3" (7.5 cm) tail of thread, string an even number of beads that will fit in a circle around this form. Make a circle of the beads by passing the needle twice through all the strung beads, exiting from the first bead strung. String one new bead and pass the needle through the third bead of the foundation round (Figure 1). String another new bead and pass the needle through the fifth bead of the foundation round. Continue around, filling in the "spaces," one bead at a time. When you reach the end of the row, you will "step down," which means that you'll pass the needle through the last bead of the foundation row, and the first bead of the row you've just worked (Figure 2).

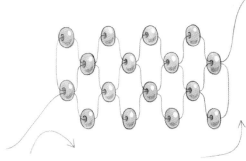

Flat peyote or one-drop peyote

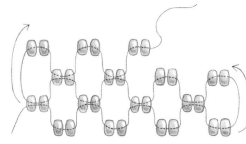

Start

Two-drop peyote

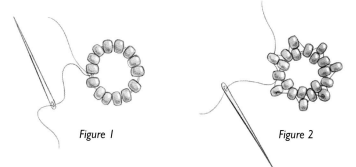

Figure 1

Figure 2

String a new bead and start the next row by skipping over one bead, pass through the second bead added in the second round and pull thread tight (Figure 3). String one bead and pass through the third bead added in the second round. Continue around, filling in the "spaces" as you did on the previous row. Exit from the first bead added in each round.

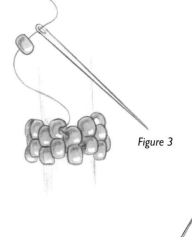

Figure 3

When you've finished your tube, weave the excess thread through three or four of the previous rows in a circular direction, tie it discreetly between two beads, and then cut it close to the knot.

Peyote stitch decreases—To make a row-end decrease, simply stop your row short and begin a new row. To make a hidden row-end decrease, pass through the last bead on a row. Weave your thread between two beads of the previous row, looping it around the thread that connects the beads. Pass back through the last bead of the row just worked and continue across in regular flat peyote.

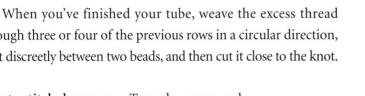

Hidden row-end decrease   *Mid-project decrease*

To make a mid-project decrease, simply pass thread through two beads without adding a bead in the "gap." In the next row, work regular one-drop peyote over the decrease. Keep tension taut to avoid holes.

Square stitch—Begin the foundation row by stringing an even number of beads. To start the second row, string one bead, pass the needle through the second-to-last bead of the foundation row (which should be directly above the newly strung bead), and then back through the bead just strung. Continue by stringing one bead, passing the needle through the bead above it and back through the bead just strung. Keep the tension on the thread snug and even. Repeat this looping technique across to the end of the row, and then pass the thread back through the last row to stabilize and reinforce it.

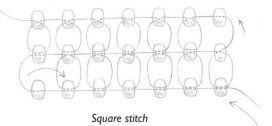

Square stitch

Start

Ladder stitch—Using two needles, one threaded on each end of the thread, pass one needle through one or more beads from left to right and pass the other needle through the same beads from right to left. Continue adding beads by criss-crossing both needles through one bead at a time. Use this stitch to make strings of beads or as the foundation for brick stitch.

Ladder stitch

Brick stitch—This technique is also known as "Comanche weave." Begin by creating a foundation row in ladder stitch (see above). String one bead and pass through the closest exposed loop of the foundation row. Pass back through the same bead and continue, adding one bead at a time.

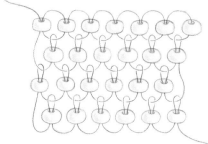

Brick stitch

Ndebele stitch (also known as herringbone weave)—This weave is often found in the beadwork of the South African Ndebele tribe. For purposes of illustration, we show alternating rows of two colors. You can, of course, use one color or any number. String 16 beads as follows: 1 light, *2 dark, 2 light; repeat from *, end strand with 1 light. Leave a 6" (15 cm) tail.

Rows 1–3: String 1 dark bead. Pass back through the last light bead strung. Skip 2 dark beads and pass through the next light bead. String 2 dark beads. Pass through the next light bead. Skip 2 dark beads. Pass through the next light bead. String 2 dark beads. Pass through the next light bead. Skip 2 dark beads. Pass through the next light bead. String 2 dark beads. Pass through the next light bead. Skip 2 dark beads. Pass through the last light bead.

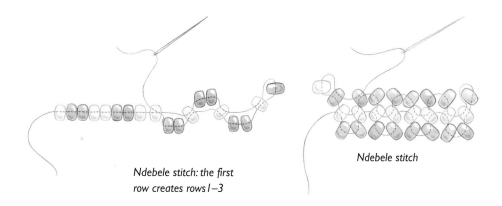

Ndebele stitch: the first row creates rows 1–3

Ndebele stitch

Row 4: String 1 dark and 1 light bead. Pass back through the dark bead just strung. *Pass through the first bead of the next 2-bead set. String 2 light beads. Pass through the next dark bead. Repeat from * until you've reached the end of the row.

Row 5: Turn work over. String 1 light bead and 1 dark bead. Pass back through the light bead just strung. *Pass through the first bead of the next 2-bead set. String 2 dark beads. Pass through the next light bead. Repeat from * to end of row.

Continue working in alternating pattern to desired length.

Bead Fringe

This is the perfect way to finish off many beadwork pieces. I'll explain several fringe methods here, and you'll find other fringe suggestions in the specific projects.

Knotted at the end—Anchor threads directly to the item, then simply string the number of beads you want on your fringe and tie a knot after exiting the last bead.
To tie a knot close to the last bead, form a loose overhand knot.

Put your needle through the knot so that it holds the thread coming out of the bead tight up against the bead. Begin pulling on the thread to tighten the knot, keeping the needle holding the thread stable against the bead. Tighten the knot, cut thread and remove the needle. Dab the knot with a spot of glue or nail polish to secure.

Knotted in the middle—String the number of beads you want on your fringe and, after exiting the last bead, pass back through the next-to-last bead and half the beads on the fringe. Tie a knot around the beaded thread at this point, cut thread and remove needle. Dab knot with glue or nail polish to secure.

Take care of your eyes

It's very important to rest your eyes periodically when beading or working bead crochet. Look away from the work, focus on a distant point, and look around a bit. This helps to prevent eye strain. Too many of us are obsessive about beading and will sit immobilized for several hours, only staggering up from our seats when our vision becomes blurred.

Knotted in the work—String the number of beads you want on your fringe and, after exiting the last bead, pass back through the next-to-last and all other beads on the fringe. Work the thread back in your work and tie it off, or move to the next position on the item to make another fringe.

Simple looped fringe —For this easily worked fringe, anchor your thread to the edge to be fringed. String a measured length of beads, form a loop, and stitch the thread next to the first anchor spot. For each successive loop, string the same length of beads and pass it through the previous loop to interlace them before stitching the loop to the edge.

Simple looped fringe

Branches—Anchor your thread to the edge to be fringed. String the number of beads you want for the main fringe length, pass back through the next-to-last and several other beads on the main stem. *Thread a few beads to make a branch, and pull them down to the main stem, pass back through the next to last and then other branch beads. Pass back through several beads on the main stem and repeat from *, this time placing the branch beads on the opposite side of the previous branch. Work back up the main stem making branches, or simply up to the edge and secure the thread. See Talisman Necklace, page 86, or Vermont Wilderness Bracelet, page 55 for illustrations of this technique.

Branch fringe

Picots—Add these bead arrangements directly to the edge to be fringed. Anchor your thread, then string one large, one medium, and one small bead, pass back through the medium and large beads to the anchor spot. For another style of picot, string one large bead, three small beads, then pass back through the large bead. The small beads will form a picot under the large bead. Picots can also be added at the lower end of simple fringe strands. See Vermont Wilderness Bracelet, page 55 for illustrations of picot fringe styles.

Picots

Projects

Spiral Swirl Earrings

These earrings are made with beaded tubular single crochet in an easy color pattern. This simple technique yields a striking result, and the earrings are a great project for those people who enjoy instant gratification.

The bead amounts listed will make one pair of earrings 2" (5 cm) long, not including ear wires.

MATERIAL

- Seed beads: 20 size 8°, in six colors: dark blue, ruby red, teal, pink, purple, lime green.
- Beads for drop: Two 8mm round crackle beads in teal; four 8°—two red, 2 purple; two 6mm oval faceted crystals.
- 1 spool blue FFF Gudebrod Silk
- 1 pair silver ear wires
- Two 6mm split jump rings

NOTIONS

- Beading needles
- Big Eye needle
- Crochet hook, size 5 (1.7 mm) steel
- Mandrel
- Needle-nose pliers
- Stitch marker or safety pin

Note: Review Crochet and Beading Tips and Techniques, and Materials and Notions chapters, pages 17 and 29, and page 11, before starting project:
Mandrel, page 27
Stringing beads, page 29
Tubular crochet, page 26

Earrings

1 *Step 1:* Make a sample of the stringing pattern as follows: Select the color order in which you plan to work your beads: A, B, C, D, E, and F. For a visual reference, thread a 12" (30.5 cm) strand of Gudebrod on a beading needle and string 1 row of beads in the order you want. Use this string as a visual reference as you work.

2 *Step 2:* String 9" (23 cm) of the color pattern on the spool of Gudebrod thread to make a tubular crochet earring 1½" (1.3 cm) long. You will be working directly from the spool.

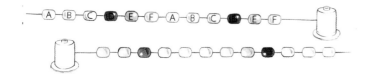

3 *Step 3:* Leaving a 6" (15 cm) tail of thread, work as follows: **Foundation row:** (without beads) Ch 6, and join into a circle with sl st. Place a stitch marker at beg of round and move the marker up when each new round begins.

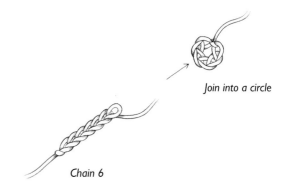

Join into a circle

Chain 6

Note: The crochet will be on the inside of the work and the beads on the outside. The hook is inserted into the stitches from the inside to the outside, and you'll be working counterclockwise if you're right-handed and clockwise if you're left-handed.

Rnds 1 and 2: Work sc in a continuous spiral fashion without beads. Place the crochet tube on a mandrel.

Rnd 3: Slide 1 bead up to the hook and sc with bead into each st to end of rnd.

4 *Step 4:* Repeat rnd 3 until the beaded tube measures about 1½" (3.8 cm). As you work, check your stringing and bead order to make sure it's the same as your sample: The colors will spiral down and around in an unbroken line, in the order strung: A, B, C, D, E, F. It's easy to forget or make a mistake while you're stringing, and it's much easier to fix such mistakes at this stage, before you finish the earring.

Step 5: When you've finished the tube, remove the mandrel. Cut thread leaving a 6" (15 cm) tail. Thread the lower 6" (15 cm) tail (from the foundation row) through the Big Eye needle; insert the needle through the tube center to the opposite end and bring the tail out through this end. This move will pull the first 2 rows of sc up into the core. Keep the tail taut, but not so tight that it makes the tube buckle or curve.

THREAD THE BOTTOM DROP BEADS

Step 6: Thread beads onto the thread tail in the following order: one 8mm teal crackle bead, one red 8°, one 6mm oval faceted crystal, and one purple 8°. Bring your needle and thread out of the last bead, skip the 8° to anchor, and then pass back through the 6mm, 8°, and 8mm beads.

Weave the thread back and forth through the tube center to secure. Trim the tail close to the work.

Step 7: Check the angle of the beads around the tube, and if any are skewed, straighten them by threading a needle through. After the thread is anchored securely, trim close to work.

Step 8: Thread the last 6" (15 cm) tail through the Big Eye needle and insert through the tube core in the opposite direction from the previous tail. Weave the thread back and forth inside the core several times to secure. Trim tail close to the work.

ATTACH BEADED TUBE TO EAR WIRE

Step 9: Open one split jump ring sideways with needle-nose pliers. Hook the ring top through the center top threads of the crochet tube. Use the pliers to open the bottom loop of the ear wire sideways, slip the jump ring on, and close both loops. Repeat Steps 1–9 to make a second earring.

Night Sky Cuff

While sitting in my studio one day, I decided to make a cuff-style bracelet with bead crochet. I was a bit timid with my first attempt, but then I quickly decided that more is better with beads. My palette was jewel tones and black, and it reminded me of a night sky with brilliant colors. Use free-form bead crochet and a medley of your favorite beads in various shapes and sizes to create your own twinkling Night Sky Cuff.

The bead amounts listed will make 1 cuff, about 1½" (3.8 cm) wide by 7" (18 cm) in length. To make a wider or longer cuff, increase the number of beads.

MATERIALS
- Seed beads: Three 6" (15 cm) tubes of 6° and 8°
- Assorted small accent beads: 20 beads of each size (6mm, 8 mm) in a mixture of triangles, magatamas, squares, teardrops, daggers, small ovals, M&Ms, small furnace glass, rondelles, 4–6mm round, Miracle beads, tubes, daggers, Balinese silver
- 1 spool black Mastex thread or color to complement your beads
- 1 button with shank

NOTIONS
- Crochet hook, size 1 (2.25 mm) steel
- Big Eye needle
- Scissors
- Nail polish or correction fluid

GAUGE
48 sc = 4" (10 cm). Adjust hook size if necessary to obtain the correct gauge.

Note: Review Crochet and Beading Tips and Techniques, pages 17 and 29, before starting this project:

Stringing beads, page 29

Flat crochet, page 31

Gauge, page 22

Cuff

1 *Step 1:* Use Mastex thread and cut the end at an angle. Stiffen the end with nail polish or correction fluid and let dry. You will be working directly from the spool.

2 *Step 2:* Using the stiffened end of Mastex, string 15" (38 cm) of assorted beads in the following sequence: two 6° seed beads, a square, a 6 or 8mm Miracle bead, two 6° seed beads, a teardrop, four 6°s, a 6mm Austrian faceted crystal, two 6°s, four 8°s, a dagger bead, a square, two 8°s, Balinese silver bead, four 6°s, a freshwater pearl, 3 magatamas, two 6°s, a small accent bead, and so on. Or string the beads in a random pattern to your liking. For a delicate look, use smaller beads: 8°s, 4–6mm cubes, tiny teardrops or daggers. You will be crocheting 3 beads at a time.

3 *Step 3:* Make a sample swatch to determine the pattern and check the width and tension. Work as follows: ***Foundation row:*** (without beads) Ch 18, ch 2 to turn.

Row 1: (with beads) Slide 3 beads up to the hook and insert hook into third ch from hook and work sc, *slide 3 beads up to the hook, sc in next ch; repeat instructions from * to end of row, ch 2 to turn.

Row 2: (without beads) Insert hook into second sc from side edge and work sc, *sc next st; repeat instructions from * to end of row, ch 2 to turn.

Row 3: (with beads) Slide 3 beads up to the hook and insert hook into second sc from side edge and work sc, *slide 3 beads up to the hook and sc in next st; repeat instructions from * to end of row, ch 2 to turn.

Repeat last 2 rows twice more, and then check the sample swatch for size, tension, and pattern.

4 *Step 4:* If you like your sample, remove the stitches and continue restringing until you have 5–6 yards (4.5–5.5 m) of strung beads. Widen the cuff by adding more chs to the foundation row or use

---

TIP BOX:

15" (38 cm) of strung beads = 1½ x 1¾" section, when crocheting 3 beads at a time. This rule does depend upon the size of the beads and how many you're crocheting at a time, so the length may vary, i.e., if you're using 1, 2, or 3 beads at a time. Work a practice swatch to decide which you prefer. For the designs in this book, I used 3 beads each time, and the instructions are written as such.

fewer chs to narrow the cuff. Your sample piece will help you decide. Remember, a wider or longer cuff will require more beads.

5 *Step 5:* Repeat Step 3, working the foundation row and rows 1 through 3. Then repeat rows 2 and 3 until the cuff is within two rows of the desired length. Work the last 2 rows without beads to create a smooth space in which to attach the button. Cut thread leaving a 4" (10 cm) tail, and with Big Eye needle weave the tail through several crochet sts on the wrong side of the work. Trim tail close to the work.

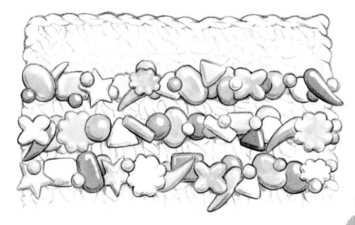

6 *Step 6:* Cut a 12" (30.5 cm) strand of Mastex and thread the Big Eye needle. Fold the thread in half to make a double strand and attach a button in the center of the smooth end (the 2 rows made without beads). Make sure the button is centered between both side edges and anchor thread to secure. Weave in loose ends through crochet stitches on the wrong side to secure.

Make the button loop

7 *Step 7:* Working directly from the spool of Mastex, leave a 4" (10 cm) tail and make a crochet chain long enough to fit snugly around the button. Don't make this ch too loose or the button will slip out. Cut thread leaving a 4" (10 cm) tail and insert through the last stitch to secure. Fold the ch in half and make sure the loop aligns with the button position at the other cuff end. Thread the needle with both tails and attach them to the cuff, working into the same stitch to attach the loop. Join the spool of Mastex at the base of the loop and work a row of sc stitches around the outside of the loop for decoration and extra strength. Cut thread and stitch into the base to secure.

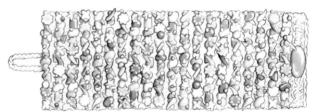

Finishing

8 *Step 8:* One at a time, thread loose ends through the beading needle and weave in through the crochet stitches on the wrong side of work to secure. Trim ends close to work.

The cuff width may expand or contract due to varying bead sizes. If this happens, take the hook or thread the Big Eye needle, and use extra beads to stitch along the outer edges for symmetry.

Cluster of Jewels

I love the natural twist of the cluster necklace. The spiral stitch rope provides a rainbow of colors, while the rich fringing of the tassel increases the overall gemlike look of the piece. Create a marvelous beaded treasure to wear like the two shown here, or explore your own creativity with your choice of beads and patterns.

The bead amounts listed will make 1 cluster necklace about 38" (96.5 cm), not including fringe.

MATERIALS
- Seed beads: 1 tube each of 6°, 8°, and 11°. *Note:* Make sure that the holes of the 11's are large enough to accommodate 4 strands of Nymo F thread
- Assorted accent beads: 20 each of triangles in different sizes, magatamas, squares, daggers, teardrops
- Assorted beads in various shapes, colors and sizes: 20 each of Balinese silver beads, furnace glass, 6–8mm round, ovals, Miracle beads, in your choice of colors
- 1 spool rose Mastex
- 1 bobbin black Nymo

NOTIONS
- Crochet hook, size 1 (2.25mm) steel
- Beeswax
- Beading needles
- Big Eye needle
- Scissors
- Nail polish or correction fluid

GAUGE
- 40 sc with beads = 4" (10 cm). Adjust hook size if necessary to obtain the correct gauge

Note: Review Crochet and Beading Tips and Techniques, pages 17 and 29, before starting the project:
Tubular crochet, page 26
Flat crochet, page 23
Fringes, page 36

Centerpiece Cluster

1 *Step 1:* Use Mastex thread and cut the end at an angle. Stiffen end with nail polish or correction fluid and let dry. You will be working directly from the spool.

2 *Step 2:* Using the stiffened end as a needle, string 24" (61 cm) of assorted beads as follows: 3 size 8s, 2 triangles, 1 square, 4mm round, 4 size 6s, 1 dagger bead, 3 squares, 2 size 8s, etc., or string beads in a random pattern to your liking.

3 *Step 3:* Make a sample swatch to determine the pattern, and size. Work as follows:
Foundation row: (without beads) Ch 30, ch 2 to turn.
Row 1: (without beads) Insert hook into third ch from hook and sc, *sc in next ch; repeat instructions from * to end of row, ch 2 to turn.
Row 2: (with beads) Slide 3 beads up to the hook and insert hook into second sc from side edge and work sc, *slide 3 beads up to the hook and sc next st; repeat instructions from * to end of row, ch 2 to turn.
Row 3: (without beads) Insert hook into second sc from side edge and work sc, *sc in next stitch; repeat instructions from * to end of row, ch 2 to turn.

Work the last 2 rows twice more and check your tension and spacing.

Note: In flat crochet, always alternate one row sc without beads, and one row sc with beads. If you forget, and work 2 rows with beads, you will know immediately since the beads will be on the wrong side. If you like the pattern, size, and style of your swatch, then continue with this piece as the cluster. If not, either put it aside for future reference, or pull the crochet out and restring the beads using another pattern. If you like what you have so far, carry on as follows:

Repeat rows 2 and 3 until the crocheted piece measures about 3" (7.5 cm) long (Figure 1). The cluster will twist slightly, which is natural (Figure 2). Cut thread leaving a 12" (30.5 cm) tail, and pull thread through last stitch to secure.

Figure 1

Figure 2

Step 4: Thread the tail through the Big Eye needle. Allowing the twist to guide you, stitch or weave both sides of the flat piece together to make a long oval tube. If some areas of the tube appear a little sparse, use extra Mastex to add strands of beads and fill in where needed. Be sure to work evenly.

Hanging Loop

This loop attaches the centerpiece cluster to the spiral rope.

Step 5: With Mastex, crochet a chain about 2–3" (5–7.5 cm) long, then double the chain into a loop and stitch it into the top of the centerpiece cluster. You can embellish the loop with beads, either by working a row of bead crochet on top of the chain, or adding beads with a needle and thread. *Note:* If your spiral rope chain is finished, and already connected together, make the chain stitch hanging loop a little larger to go around the spiral rope, and then attach it at the bottom of the center-piece cluster.

Fringes

Use a variety of beads to make your fringe strands. The fringes in my necklaces have loops of accent beads and straight strands of 3 or 4 large beads strung together, or strands of seed beads, charms, spacers, flower-shaped beads, hummingbirds, and leaves.

Step 6: Cut 5 ft (152.5 cm) of Nymo F and thread it on beading needle. Fold thread in half, wax well, then attach the double strand to the base of the crochet cluster, leaving a 6" (15 cm) tail to weave in later. Make 4 to 6 beaded fringe strands in staggered lengths, using patterns of your choosing. My fringes range from 2¾–3½" (7–9 cm) long. Attach each stranded fringe to the base of the centerpiece by inserting the needle and thread through a crochet stitch once or twice, then move the needle over one stitch, and attach the next fringe. When the final strand is attached to the base of the cen-terpiece cluster, weave the thread end through the crochet stitches on the inside side of the center-piece cluster to secure. Weave in the beginning 6" (15 cm) tail through the center of the cluster to secure. Trim ends close to work.

Spiral Rope Chain

I learned this stitch some time ago, and unfortunately, can't remember whom to credit. Start with two contrasting colors of seed beads. Using two high-contrast colors makes it easy to see and understand what you're doing. You'll be working with core beads and outside beads. I've alternated and changed my two contrasting colors often, so my spiral rope has many colors.

Step 7: Cut and wax about 9–10 ft (3–4 m) of Nymo F thread. You will be working with a double strand for strength.

Step 8: Pick up and thread 4 core 8° beads and 3 outside 8° beads (Figure 1). Pull all 7 beads down to the bottom of the thread, leaving a 6" (15 cm) tail, which will be woven in later. The 8° beads are easy to see and make the pattern more visible. As you become more comfortable with the stitch pattern, you can switch to 11° beads, alternating with 8°s. If the 11° bead holes are too small, and the threads can't pass through a bead several times, simply add a bead or two on a strand

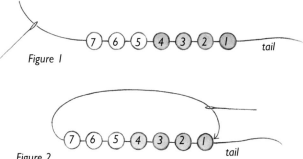

Figure 1

Figure 2

of Nymo, and attach them on the outside of the pattern to avoid threading through the same hole several times.

Step 9: Pass your needle back through the 4 core beads from right to left, (Figure 2) with the needle coming out of bead #4, and pull thread tight, forming an irregular loop with the core beads on the bottom and the outside beads (#5–6–7) on top (Figure 3). The beading process will look a little strange at this

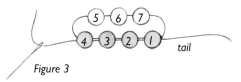

Figure 3

point, but don't be concerned, it's supposed to be like that.

Step 10: Pick up 1 core bead (#8) and 3 outside beads (#9–10–11) and draw them down to the work so the five core beads form an unbroken line (Figure 4). Skip core bead #1 and pass needle through core beads #2–3–4

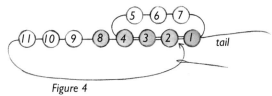

Figure 4

and #8, and outside beads #9–10–11. The core beads (#1–2–3–4–8) are sitting in the center, with the outside beads (#5–6–7) above the core beads, and the other outside beads (#9–10–11) below the core beads (Figure 5).

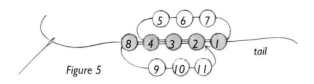

Figure 5

tail

Step 11: Pick up one core bead (#12), and three outside beads (#13–14–15), pull the new beads down to the work, skip core beads #1 and 2, and pass needle through core beads #3–4–8–12 (Figure 6).

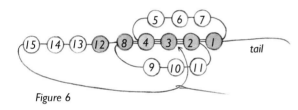

tail

Figure 6

Step 12: Repeat steps 10 and 11, continuing to add one new core bead and three outside beads each time. Skip one core bead and pass the needle through 4 core beads and the new outside beads each time. This creates the spiraling effect. Change colors and bead sizes as you wish, until the chain is the desired length. My chains are about 34" (86.5 cm) long.

Step 13: Slip the spiral rope chain through the crocheted hanging loop and tie the thread ends together with a square knot. Seal the knot with nail polish. When polish is dry, weave the thread tails back into the spiral to strengthen and hide the join. Trim tail close to the work.

Vermont Wilderness Bracelet

I created this bracelet cuff during our first winter in Vermont. It was bitterly cold, with lots of snow, and as I sat in the snug, cozy living room, looking out big windows into the snowy white woods and lake below, the monochromatic winter scene inspired me to create something with lots of color. This design combines fiber and beads of many shapes, brilliant color, riotous fringe, and lavish edgings. If you love gorgeous, trendy yarns, and beads, this design gives you an ideal opportunity to create a striking bracelet.

The bead amounts listed will make a 2" (5 cm) wide × 6½" (16.5 cm) long bracelet. Measurements do not include fringes.

MATERIALS
- Seed Beads: One 6" (15 cm) tube of each size, 6° and 8°
- Assorted accent beads: 6–10mm, various accent beads in different sizes, glass donuts, small charms, about 20–30 of each bead type
- Yarns: 30–50 grams of 3 or 4 yarns in different weights, fingering, sport, DK. The yarn combinations are held together and worked as one (see Yarn Resources, page 121)
- Button: 1" (2.5 cm) diameter, purchased, or make a small crochet cluster of assorted beads
- 1 spool black Mastex thread
- 1 bobbin black Nymo F

NOTIONS
- Crochet hook H/6 (5.5 mm). Your hook size will depend on your choice of yarns. Work a swatch to determine the size that works best with your yarn selections.
- Beading needle
- Big Eye needle
- Beeswax

GAUGE:
- 16 beaded sc = 4" (10 cm). Adjust hook size if necessary to obtain the correct gauge.

Note: Review Crochet and Beading Tips and Techniques, pages 17 and 29, before starting the project:

Flat (one-drop) peyote stitch, page 32

Framing, page 30

Fringes, page 36

Turning chain, page 21

Bracelet

1 *Step 1:* Choose 3–4 yarns that coordinate with your beads. The yarns are grouped together and used as one, and they are visible on the right side of the bracelet, between the bead rows. Make sure your yarn choices are not too thick or heavy or they'll overpower the beads. You'll be working lengthwise so the foundation ch must be long enough to circle the wrist.

2 *Step 2:* Using Mastex thread and a Big Eye needle, string 80" (203 cm) of the larger size beads (6–10 mm) in the following pattern: one 6°, one 8mm Miracle bead, one 6°, three 6°s, 2 teardrops, one 10mm, one oval, one 6°, 2 squares, 3 magatamas, one rondelle, one 8mm Miracle bead, one rondelle, a glass donut, 2 daggers, 1 Balinese silver. Or string beads in a random pattern of your choosing. String the beads in groups of 3, using the framing technique of small beads on either side of a big bead. You will be crocheting 3 beads at a time and working from the spool. The finished length of strung Mastex depends on the size of the wearer's wrist. My wrist measures 6½" (16.5 cm), and I strung 26" (66 cm) to work 1 row of sc

with beads to fit around my wrist; 26" (66 cm) × 3 rows with beads = 78" (198 cm), which I rounded up to 80" (203 cm). Make a small sample to determine how many inches of strung beads it takes to work 1" (2.5 cm) of sc with beads, then multiply that number by the wearer's wrist measurement × 3 (rows). Add an inch or two extra when stringing the beads to be sure you have enough.

3 *Step 3:* Once you've strung a bead pattern, work a ***Sample Swatch*** with your yarns and beads to determine the size, tension, and pattern. If you like what you have in your sample, then continue stringing the length you need. If not, remove the crochet and try another pattern or hook size.

4 *Step 4:* For my bracelet, I worked ch 26, ch 2 for turning ch. The chain should just circle your wrist, meeting at either end, but not overlapping. Take one strand of each yarn and hold together as one, then work as follows: ***Foundation row:*** (without beads) Work the number of chs needed to circle your wrist, then ch 2 for turning ch.

Row 1: (without beads) Insert hook into third ch from hook, work sc, *sc in next ch; rep instructions from * to end of row, ch 2 to turn. Check your tension, you may need to add or subtract stitches, depending how tightly you work.

Row 2: (with beads) Using the yarns and the strung Mastex held together as one, work as follows: Slide 3 beads up to the hook, insert hook into second sc from side edge and work sc, *slide 3 beads up to hook and sc in next st; repeat instructions from * to last 2 sc, work these 2 sts with Mastex and yarns, but without adding beads, ch 2 to turn. The 2 sts worked without beads on each bead row will serve as the area on which to add the button.

Row 3: (without beads) Insert hook into second sc from edge and work sc, *sc in next st; repeat instructions from * to end of row, ch 2.

Row 4: (with beads) Slide 3 beads up to the hook, insert hook into 2nd sc from side edge and work sc, *slide 3 beads up to the hook and sc in next st; repeat instructions from * to last 2 sts, work 2 sc without beads, ch 2 to turn.

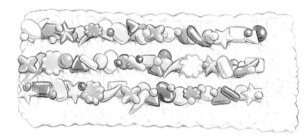

Repeat rows 3 and 4, alternating a nonbead row with a bead row until bracelet is desired width. Work a nonbead row to end bracelet width. My bracelet is 2" (5 cm) wide and has 3 bead rows. Cut yarns and Mastex, leaving a 6" (15 cm) tail of each; pull all tails through the last loop to secure st. Working one yarn tail at a time, thread the Big Eye needle and weave tails through crochet sts on wrong side of work.

Fringes

My fringes are different on each side. The fringes can include branches, loops, or single strands of beads along one long edge of the bracelet, and all single beads with picots along the other edge. Make the fringes as thick or fine as you like.

5 *Step 5:* Cut 9 ft (2.74 m) of waxed Nymo F and thread your beading needle, fold thread in half to make a double strand. Tie thread to one end of the crocheted piece, leaving a 4" (15 cm) tail to be woven in at the end, then begin the fringes. See illustration for sample ideas.

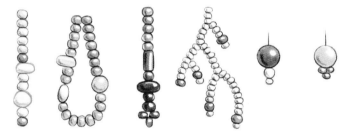

Button Clasp

6 *Step 6:* You can either purchase a button with a shank or make a beaded one using bead crochet. To create a bead crochet button, string 24" (61 cm) of beads on Mastex thread. Crochet a small square using sc and working 2 or 3 beads into each st every other row. With Mastex thread, sew running sts around the edges of the square. Next, pull the thread and gather the edges to create an oval or circle; whipstitch the edges together to close. Attach your button clasp onto the bracelet

end without beads. Center the clasp between the
side edges.

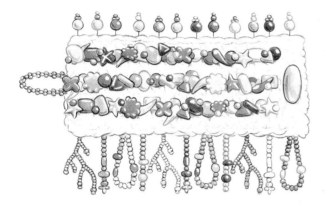

Loop

Step 7: Use Mastex directly from the spool, leaving a 4" (10 cm) tail, and make a ch long enough
to loop over your button clasp. The fit should be
snug. Cut thread, leaving a 4" (10 cm) tail and
insert through last ch to secure. Fold ch in half to
form a loop and thread both 4" (10 cm) yarn tails
on Big Eye needle and attach both to the opposite
end of the bracelet from the button, aligning the
loop with the button. Stitch the loop firmly in
place and weave the tails through the crochet sts
on the wrong side of the bracelet to secure.
Optional: If you prefer, make a peyote st loop and
attach as above.

Finishing

Step 8: Thread any loose tails on the Big Eye needle, one at a time, and weave through crochet sts
on wrong side of work to secure.

Classic and Not-So-Classic Bead Crochet Ropes and Bracelet

The instructions here include two beaded crochet ropes and a bracelet. The classic rope style is worked in slip-stitch bead crochet, and the not-so-classic rope is worked in single crochet bead crochet, and is also shown in a bracelet. The techniques produce two different looks, so experiment to see which one you prefer.

Classic Bead Crochet Rope

The first design is a classic bead crochet rope that dates back to the 1920s with a sleek, smooth, and timeless shape. It worked well with Jazz Era drop-waist dresses and cloche hats, and it works equally well with the fashion styles of the twenty-first century.

The bead amounts listed will make one a 24" (61 cm) slip-stitch necklace.

MATERIALS FOR SLIP-STITCH NECKLACE
- Seed Beads: 4 tubes 6°, 2 tubes each of 4 colors of your choice
- Assorted accent beads: 1 or 2 glass leaves, a few 11°s. Optional: large lampworked or furnace bead with a large hole
- 1 spool blue Mastex, or color to complement your bead colors

NOTIONS
- Crochet hook, size 2 (2.5mm) steel
- Big Eye needle
- Nail polish or correction fluid
- Scissors

Note: Review Crochet and Beading Tips and Techniques, pages 17 and page 29, before starting the project:
Slip stitch crochet, page 21
Tubular crochet, page 26
Tubular peyote stitch, page 33
Flat (one-drop) peyote stitch, page 32

Slip-Stitch Necklace: Classic Bead Crochet Rope

1 *Step 1:* Use Mastex thread and cut the end at an angle. Stiffen with nail polish or correction fluid and let dry. Using the stiffened end as a needle, string the beads one at a time onto the Mastex spool in A-B-C-D sequence (one letter for each color). Note that 5½" (14 cm) of strung 6's equals about 1" (2.5 cm) of slip-stitch bead crochet. To make a 24" (61 cm) necklace, string 132" (335.5 cm) or 11 ft (3.35 m).

2 *Step 2:* Make a slipknot in the Mastex thread, leaving a 6" (15 cm) tail. **Foundation row:** Ch 4, inserting one bead into each ch in color formation A-B-C-D. Join ch into circle with sl st. The crochet will be on the inside of the work and the beads on the outside. Insert the hook into the sts from the inside to the outside, working counterclockwise if you're right-handed and clockwise if you're left-handed.

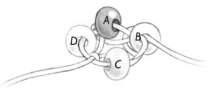

3 *Step 3:* Turn the first bead sideways, so the hole is positioned north and south, and hold it in place. Insert the hook through the upper thread stitch

loop; you now have 2 strands on the hook. Pull down corresponding color bead, hold it *behind* the hook, yo and pull the loop through both threads on hook—1 loop on hook. As you complete the stitch, the lower bead will stay on its side, locked into place by the thread. The bead you've just added—the *new* bead—will be standing up, with the hole in north-south position. This maneuver is a little tricky at the beginning, but have faith; the different colors and letters will help to keep you on track. After you've done about 4 rows, you'll be able to see the pattern and follow it. If you make a mistake, simply pull it out and start over. You *will* have an "ah-ha!" moment when it all works and makes sense.

4 *Step 4:* Repeat step 3 until the rope is the desired length. To finish, work a row of sl st *without* beads to make a 4-bead circle with all the beads lying on their sides.

5 *Step 5:* To join ends, tie the thread tails into a square knot. Thread one tail on a Big Eye needle, and weave through the beads, hiding the join. Trim the tail close to the work. Thread the other tail and weave through the beads in the opposite

This is the center peyote stitch bead on the classic rope necklace

direction and trim as before. **Option:** Slide a lampworked, furnace, dichroic, or other glass bead (it must have a large hole) over the crochet rope, and weave thread back and forth through the bead hole, stitching the thread back into the bead crochet rope to hide it. For my necklace, I made a flat peyote st rectangle, which I then sewed into a tube. Using 6° seed beads, string an even number of beads to encircle the rope and begin working one-drop peyote st (see page 32). Continue working peyote st until you have a flat

piece about 2½" (6.5 cm) long. Fold the piece in half and stitch the edges to make a tube. If you wish, embellish the tube with a few random beads across the top. Slide the tube onto the rope and stitch it in place at both ends.

Classic Bead Crochet Rope

Classic and Not-So-Classic Bead Crochet Rope and Bracelet

Not-So-Classic Single Crochet Bead Rope and Bracelet

The bead amounts listed will make one necklace rope 28" (71 cm) long, with the upper 8" (20.5 cm) worked in single crochet only, without beads. The bracelet is 8" (20.5 cm).

MATERIALS

- Seed Beads: 2 tubes each of 8° and 6°
- Assorted accent beads: 1–2 tubes each of the cubes and magatamas, 20–40 beads in 4mm size, and 20–40 small Miracle beads

Mix all the beads in a bead spinner to make bead soup. Because the design is free-form and depends entirely upon personal preference, the bead amounts listed are only approximations. I used a variety of colors, including purple, lavender, mauve, green, silver, and turquoise.

- 1 spool twisted pearl cotton thread in purple, or a color to complement your beads

NOTIONS

- Crochet hook size 2 (2.5mm) steel
- Bead spinner with curved needle
- Mandrel
- Big Eye needle
- Scissors

Note: Review Crochet and Beading Tips and Techniques, and Materials and Notions chapters, pages 17, 29, and page 11, before starting the project:
Tubular crochet, page 26
Mandrel, page 27

Necklace

1 *Step 1:* Pour the beads into the bead spinner; using the curved needle, twirl the spinner and scoop up the beads. Bead spinners are fun to use, but they may take a little practice to get used to. It's very satisfying to watch the beads slide effortlessly up the needle. You will need about 5" (12.5 cm) of strung 8's to make 1" (2.5 cm) of tubular bead crochet.

2 *Step 2:* **Foundation row:** Leaving a 6" (15 cm) tail, make a slipknot and ch 6, inserting a bead into each ch. Join into circle with a slip st.

Rnd 1: (with beads) *Slip 3 beads up to the hook and work sc in one st; repeat instructions from * to end of round—6 sts. Slip sc ring onto the mandrel.

Leaving work on the mandrel, repeat rnd 1 working in continuous rnds without joining or turning until the necklace is desired length. I stopped working rounds with beads after 20" (51 cm) and finished the necklace back working sc with pearl thread only. Tubular single crochet is a pretty stitch that looks nice on its own.

Finishing

3 *Step 3:* Cut the pearl thread leaving a 6" (15 cm) tail and thread the Big Eye needle. Connect the necklace ends by weaving the yarn tail through the beads at the beginning of the foundation row; work the yarn tail back and forth through the beads several times to secure. If needed, add a few extra beads to disguise the join. Thread the foundation row tail on the Big Eye needle and weave back and forth through the crochet sts to secure. Trim tails close to the work.

Bracelet

To make the bracelet, work using the same technique as the Not-so-Classic necklace until the rope measures 8" (20.5 cm), then finish off the same as the necklace, weaving tails through beads and crochet core to join. Trim tails close to the work. The bracelet shown uses 6's and is crocheted using one bead at a time, not 3 as in the other designs.

Spirit Box

The idea for the Spirit Box originated at a meeting of a 12-step program. I learned that fears or problems that one has difficulty letting go of can be given to a higher power (God, Goddess, Buddha, or Whomever) by writing the situation on a slip of paper, folding it, and placing it in a Spirit or God Box with a silent or spoken request that one let the situation go and turn it over to God. The physical act of writing the situation down and giving it away helps one detach from it.

In the Spirit Box workshop, we all talked about life's challenges, of fear, loss, anger, faith and spirituality, and the box became a useful active tool for living. My Spirit Box is made with beads, crochet and fiber, but use your favorite media to make your box meaningful for you. Instructions for my Spirit Box follow, but you should explore and experiment with materials and ideas that are meaningful to you.

The following materials will make a circular box with lid, about 3" in diameter by 2½" deep.

MATERIALS

- Seed Beads: small amounts of 6°s, 8°s, 11°s
- Assorted accent beads: Balinese silver, cubes, triangles, other accent beads in different sizes

  Special small objects and/or beads with meaning to you: childhood charms or amulets, buttons, gifts, fetishes, fabric, stones, glass, beads, etc.
- Yarns: 30–50 grams of 3 or 4 yarns in different weights; fingering, sport, DK. The yarn combinations are held together and worked as one.
- 1 spool complementary-colored Mastex
- 1 bobbin Nymo F

NOTIONS

- Crochet hook, size F (4 mm)
- Beading needles
- Beeswax
- Big Eye needle
- Small ruler or measuring tape
- Scissors

Note: Review Crochet and Beading Tips and Techniques, pages 17 and 29, before starting project:
Tubular crochet, page 26
Circular flat crochet, page 24

Box Base and Body

 Step 1: With a Big Eye needle, string 2½–3 yards (2.28–2.75 m) of beads on the spool of Mastex and set aside until later. Select the yarns and hold a strand of each together as one yarn.

 *Step 2:* This piece employs circular crochet, both flat and dimensional. The base is worked without beads.
Foundation row for base: Leaving a 4" (10 cm) tail, ch 4. Join into a circle with a sl st. Begin working in continuous rnds from this point.
Rnd 1: Sc in each ch to end of rnd.
Rnd 2: (increases) Work 2 sc in each sc—8 sc.
Rnd 3: Work sc each st—8 sts.

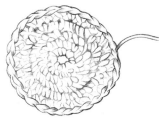 *Step 3:* Repeat Rnds 2 and 3, working increases as needed to maintain even edges until the base is the desired radius. My base measures about 3" (7.5 cm) across the center.

SIDES

 Step 4: When the base is the desired width, begin the sides. If you want to use another color for the sides, or another group of yarns, change them before you begin the sides. Repeat rnd 3 only, sc in each st and working in a spiral fashion without further increases. Add stranded Mastex to the yarns and work one or two beads in the sc sts, using a random pattern. Keep your tension firm to give the box a strong structure.

Step 5: When the sides reach the desired height, cut the yarns and Mastex leaving 4" (10 cm) tails and weave the fibers back into the body on the wrong side of the work.

Box Top

Step 6: With Mastex, thread the beads in a random pattern in groups of 3 beads. You will need 36" (91.5 cm) of beads.

Step 7: Hold the yarns and the strung Mastex thread together as one. The top is made in circular crochet with increases, just like the base.

Foundation Row: (without beads) Work same as in step 2 above.

Rnd 1: (no beads) *Work 2 sc in each ch; repeat from * to end of rnd.

Rnd 2: *Slip 3 beads up to the hook work sc; repeat from* to end of rnd.

Rnd 3: (no beads) Sc in each st to end of rnd, working increases as needed.

Repeat rnds 2 and 3 until the top is the desired size and fits snugly on the base. My top measures about 3¾" (22 cm) and is a little curved.

Embellishment

8 *Step 8:* Cut about 9 ft (2.74 m) of Nymo F, thread a Big Eye needle, fold thread in half and use doubled. Wax thread well. Tie ends in a double or triple knot, weave the needle in and out around the box, making your own design and embellishing as you work. Add your beads, charms, or whatever pleases you. You can string small sections of similar size beads or frame a big bead with 2 smaller ones. You can completely cover the box or insert a few beads in strategic places.

More embellishments can be added to the top of the box in the same fashion.

Finishing

Working loose tails one at a time, thread a Big Eye needle and weave the tail in to the wrong side of the work, and through several crochet sts to secure. Trim the tails close to the work.

Box Contents

And, last but not least, take a piece of paper, cut or tear it into little strips, and start writing. Your issues can be situations at work, at home, with relatives, spouses, children, animals, politics, the planet, people you love or hate—all can be given to your Higher Power to take care of, and thereby take the burden off you! As you place your issues in the box, just say a quick prayer or request for help with the issue, and then put it out of your mind. The box may not work instantly (unfortunately), but it does work over time, regardless of whether the outcome is what you wanted. When the issue comes to mind, just remind yourself that you've put it in the box and given it to your Higher Power, ask for the right outcome—whatever that may be—and let it go.

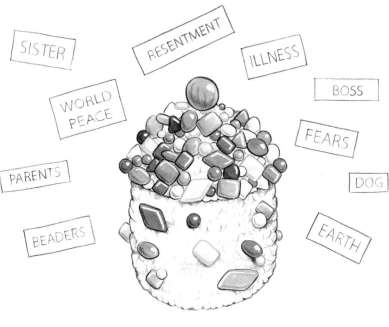

Patchwork Beaded Collar

This unique design has its origins in my love of the wonderful old crazy-quilt patchwork patterns. The Patchwork Collar combines different bead sizes and shapes with free-form flat bead crochet and peyote, brick, Ndebele, and square stitches to create a tapestry of color and texture.

The bead amounts make one 24" (61 cm) collar. The two collars shown are 20" (51 cm) and 24" (61 cm) long.

MATERIALS
- Seed Beads: 2 tubes each, 6°, 8° and 11° seed beads
- Assorted accent beads: 20 each, 6–10mm
- Small accent beads: 1 small tube each of triangle beads, magatamas, squares, 8° hexes, teardrops, twenty tiny daggers, twelve 4-6mm Austrian crystals, twelve small charms. Select beads in any colors you choose.
- 1 spool each of red, blue, black Mastex, or colors to complement your beads
- 1 bobbin black Nymo F
- Closure: 1" (2.5 cm) decorative button with shank

NOTIONS
- Crochet hook, size 0 (3.25 mm) steel
- Big Eye needle
- Beading needles
- Beeswax
- Scissors
- Nail polish or correction fluid

GAUGE
- 40 sc with beads = 4" (10 cm) Adjust hook size if necessary to obtain the correct gauge.

Note: Review Crochet and Beading Tips and Techniques, pages 17 and 29, before starting the project:
Brick st, page 35
Flat crochet, page 31

Beaded Crochet Rectangles

1 *Step 1:* Use Mastex thread in color to complement your beads, and cut the end at an angle. Stiffen the end with nail polish or correction fluid and let dry. You will be working directly from the spool. Repeat this process with each Mastex color you intend to use.

2 *Step 2:* Plan your bead-stringing pattern before you start, deciding which arrangement to string on each Mastex color, or follow the pattern listed below. Using the stiffened end of Mastex, string 20" (51 cm) of assorted beads. You will be crocheting 3 beads at a time using a framing method of 2 smaller beads on each side of a larger one, or 3 small beads together. Work as follows: String one 8°, one square, one 8°, one rondelle, 4mm Miracle bead, one rondelle, three 8°s, one teardrop, a 6mm Austrian faceted crystal, one teardrop, three 6°s, one dagger bead, one square, one dagger, one 8°, one oval, one 8°, three 8°s, three Miracle rondelles, three squares, and so on.

3 *Step 3:* Make a sample swatch to determine the pattern and size of each rectangle. Work as follows: ***Foundation row:*** (without beads) Ch 10, ch 2 to turn.

Row 1: (without beads) Insert hook into third ch from hook and sc, *sc in next ch; repeat instructions from * to end of row, ch 2 to turn.

Row 2: (with beads) Slide 3 beads up to the hook and insert hook into second sc from side edge and work sc, *slide 3 beads up to the hook and sc in next st; repeat instructions from * to end of row, ch 2 to turn.

Row 3: (without beads) Insert hook into second sc from side edge and work sc; *sc in next st; repeat instructions from * to end of row, ch 2 to turn.

Work the last 2 rows until piece measures 1½–1¾" (3.8–4.5 cm) in length. Check the gauge and pattern. Your swatch should measure about 1" (2.5 cm) in width. If not, adjust the number of sts, adding more if the swatch is too narrow, fewer if the swatch is too wide. Assuming your sample swatch is the size and width you want, cut the thread leaving a 6"(15 cm) tail to weave in later, and pull through the last loop on the hook to prevent the crochet from unraveling.

4 *Step 4:* Repeat step 3 until you have 5 beaded crochet pieces each 1" (2.5 cm) wide by 1½"–1¾" (3.8–4.5 cm) long for the shorter necklace, or 7 beaded crochet pieces for the longer version. Choose one for the focal point in the center front.

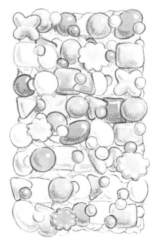

Flat Squares and Triangles

Step 5: Make 6 or 8 small, flat bead pieces using your choice of off-loom beadweaving techniques: peyote, brick, Ndebele, or square stitch. My collars use peyote st, brick st, Ndebele, and square st, and each section is 1" (2.5 cm) wide by 1½" (3.8 cm) long. The number of finished squares will depend on the size of your finished collar; make more squares for a long collar, fewer for a short collar. Work as follows: Cut 9 ft (3 m) of Nymo F

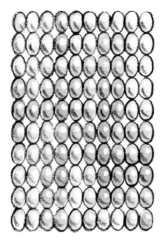

and thread it on a beading needle. Wax the thread well before stringing. Using 6° and 8° seed beads, or square beads, work each piece with your chosen method of off-loom weaving. The base of my peyote squares used 16 size 8° seed beads (illustration shows 10 beads across).

6 *Step 6:* You'll need at least two triangle sections to contour the collar. These sections are inserted on each side at the back of the neck before the final squares are attached. You can also make 2 extra triangles to place on each side of your center-front crochet piece. To make the triangles, I used 8° seed beads and a 1-drop brick stitch. Make a 2-bead ladder base, then take the needle and slide on one bead. Position the bead so that it sits above the two beads below. Needle back and insert through one of the 2 base beads. Continue increasing one extra bead at each end of every

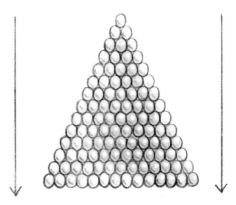

row to create a triangle. I used 14 size 8° seed beads at the base of my triangles. The triangles will connect the squares of bead crochet together and soften the angles so the collar fits comfortably around your neck.

7 *Step 7:* Lay out your design of crochet beaded pieces and flat woven pieces and insert triangles to contour the necklace. Thread the Big Eye needle with Nymo F and stitch the pieces together. Weave the thread in between the beads to secure, then cut and seal the end with nail polish. Trim the tail close to the work.

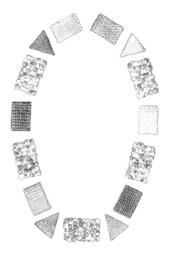

Button and Loop Closure

8 *Step 8:* Decide where to place your closure button on the back neck square, so that the collar fits comfortably around your neck, and the back neck squares are aligned. Attach the button with a strand of Mastex thread. *Loop closure:* Using a strand of Nymo F, well waxed, and leaving 6" (15 cm) thread tails to secure later, string enough size 8° seed beads (in your choice of colors) to make a loop that fits snugly around the button. Work 2 or 3 rows of peyote st around the loop, then take the thread all the way around the inner bead loop to strengthen it. Make sure the loop is neither too tight nor too loose. Trim the tail close to the work.

Embellishments

9 *Step 9:* If you wish, add charms, wirework, extra beads, or strands of beads across the tops of the flat bead sections. Thread a beading needle with a double strand of waxed Nymo F and tie the ends in an overhand knot to secure. Insert the needle through the wrong side of the work to the right side, and add the extra beads on top of the flat sections to make a pattern; you can also add beads in a free-form manner. Take the needle to the wrong side and secure the embellishments by weaving the thread through several beads and crochet pieces several times.

Finishing

10 *Step 10:* With beading needle, weave in any loose thread tails through bead sections or crochet sts to secure. Trim tail close to the work.

Bewitched and Bewoven Bijouterie

An adventure in tubular, free-form bead crochet and knotting, this design emerged when I discovered how to make bead crochet beads. They are completely addictive. When these beads are combined with multiple strands of knotting and weaving, the resulting bijouterie weaves a magical spell on both maker and admirers; hence the title.

The bead amounts listed will make one 28" (71 cm) necklace.

MATERIALS
- Seed beads: 2–3 small tubes each 6° and 8°
- Assorted accent beads: triangles, squares, magatamas. 20–30 each tiny hearts, small flat ovals, 4mm–6mm Miracle and fiber optics, small flower beads, miracle rondelles, and other small beads of your choosing
- Assortment of beads for neck-piece: 6–8 each of furnace glass, 4–8mm round, leaves, rondelles, Balinese silver, tubes, Miracle beads, 8–12 small charms
- 2 spools Mastex thread, coordinate two colors to go with your beads, because the thread is visible throughout the necklace strap

NOTIONS
- Crochet hook, size 2 (2.5 mm) steel
- Nail polish or correction fluid
- T-pins for knotting
- Big Eye needle in 2½" (6.5 cm) and 5" (12.5 cm) sizes
- Macramé board, foam core, cork-board, or anything you can stick pins into

Note: Review Crochet and Beading Tips and Techniques, Materials and Notions chapters, pages 17, 29, and page 11, before starting the project:
Single crochet, page 20
Slip stitch crochet, page 21
Tubular crochet, page 26
Mandrel, page 27

Stringing beads to make crochet beads

1 *Step 1:* Using one of your chosen Mastex thread colors, cut the end of the thread at an angle, and dip the end in nail polish or correction fluid and let dry. You may have to repeat the process several times until the end becomes stiff enough to use as a threading needle. You will be working directly from the spool of Mastex.

2 *Step 2:* Choose the size and number of accent beads you'll use in your necklace. To make the bead crochet beads, plan your own random pattern using 8's, 6's, triangles, magatamas, rondelles, 4–6mms. Here are some estimates for your reference.

MEDIUM SIZE BEAD CROCHET BEADS:

30" (76 cm) of strung Mastex will produce 3" (7.5 cm) of bead crochet to make 2 medium beads
20" (51 cm) of strung beads = one 2" (5 cm) crochet bead
15" (38 cm) of strung beads = one 1½" (3.8 cm) crochet bead

SHORT, SMALL BEADS:

12" (30.5 cm) of 6's, 8's, daggers, teardrops, magatamas, rondelles, 4–6mms, but no larger beads

For the first necklace, I used one large centerpiece tube bead in the front, one small bead on each side of the knotted necklace strap placed about midway between the front centerpiece and the back neck, and finished the back neck section with a 2" (5 cm) crochet bead tube. For the second necklace, I used a slightly smaller centerpiece

crochet tube, one medium-size crochet bead on each side about 2" (5 cm) up from the centerpiece, and a smaller bead about 2½" (6.5 cm) from the medium bead; I then finished the back neck with another medium bead. The centerpiece of both necklaces is a 56" (142 cm) beaded strand, which makes a crochet tube bead about 6½ and 7" (16.5 and 18 cm) long and uses many bead sizes, including larger ones. You will be crocheting 3 beads at a time, so consider that bulk when you are stringing beads. Try to be consistent with bead sizes to avoid making one section larger than another. Don't cut the thread, and be sure to keep your crochet beads on a mandrel until you're ready to use them.

Making the crochet beads

3 *Step 3:* Working directly from the spool of Mastex and with a crochet hook, leave a 6" (15 cm) tail and work **Foundation row:** (without beads) Ch 6, join into circle with slip st .

Rounds 1 and 2: Place the circle of stitches on the mandrel and work 2 rounds of plain single crochet without beads. It may be helpful to tape the thread tail on the dowel so it is

out of the way; taping will also help hold the piece in place. Make sure that you are working counterclockwise if you're right-handed, or clockwise if you're left-handed, otherwise the beads will be on the inside of the tube. Insert the hook from the inside to the outside of the round. Keep the stitches and tension somewhat loose but even. The mandrel will be between you and the hook, and you will be crocheting *behind* the dowel, not in front of it.

Round 3: Working in continuous rounds, without turning or joining with slip st, *slide 3 beads up to the hook and sc; rep from * in each stitch. If you miss a stitch here and there, it won't be visible, so you don't need to be precise.

4 *Step 4:* Repeat Rnd 3 until bead is the size you want to use. To end the bead, cut the thread leaving a 4" (10 cm) tail. Weave the tail through the beads and to the wrong side of the crochet to secure. Make as many crochet beads as you want for your necklace. Leave the crochet beads on the mandrel until you're ready to use them, otherwise the centers can collapse or become distorted, and it will be difficult to string them.

Center Crochet Bead Tube

5 *Step 5:* String 56" (142 cm) of beads on Mastex thread, using furnace glass, 8–10mm, Balinese silver, donuts, 8°s and 6°s; continue working in groups of 3 beads. Try to space the larger beads about every inch or two so they won't overlap when crocheted. Use a variety of large, medium, and small beads to make the centerpiece distinctive.

6 *Step 6:* **Foundation Row:** Work the same as for the crochet beads above.

Rnd 1: Slip the circle onto a mandrel, and begin 1 rnd of sc, without beads, working counterclockwise (clockwise if you're left-handed) as described in the previous section.

Rnd 2: *Slide 3 beads up to the hook and sc in next st; repeat from * to end of rnd.

Repeat rnd 2 until the tube measures about 7" (18 cm). Cut the thread, leaving a 10" (25.5 cm) tail and thread through the last st to secure. To make your centerpiece tube more free-form, increase the number of stitches as you work around the circle, i.e., instead of working one sc in each of the 6 stitches, work 2, 3, or 4 sc in each st to create interesting little bulges and shapes. You can safely remove this tube from the mandrel because you don't need the hole.

Knotted Neckpiece

7

Step 7: Cut 4 strands of Mastex, each measuring 45" (114.5 cm) long. I used 2 strands of each color. Take one strand, and use the crochet hook or the Big-Eye needle to thread the strand halfway through one of the stitches at the tube end. Fold the strand in half, so that you now have a double strand of Mastex about 22½" (57 cm) long. Thread the other 3 strands the same as the first, spacing them evenly around the end of the tube. All 4 strands are now doubled in half—8 strands total. Cut another 4 strands the same as before, and repeat the process at the other end of the center tube. Using T-pins, tack the strands into place on the macramé, foam core, or corkboard so the strands remain stationary.

8

Step 8: Work one side of the necklace at a time. With an overhand knot, secure all 8 strands together, close to the centerpiece crochet bead. Pin the strands on the board with a T-pin. Cut the strand ends at an angle and stiffen them with nail polish or correction fluid. Plan the way you want to frame your center crochet bead tube: If you're using furnace glass, glass donuts, Balinese silver, or other beads with holes large enough to cover the knot, thread them on now and knot again.

9

Step 9: Place 7 strands to one side and tack them on the board away from the remaining (8th) strand. Begin work with this strand; make a

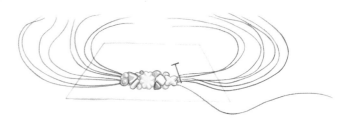

simple overhand knot close to the larger overhand knot. Thread a small bead, make another overhand knot, leave a ¼" (6 mm) space of thread, make another knot, thread three 8°s, make a knot, leave another thread space, make a knot, thread 2 small beads, make a knot, and continue working up the strand until you've worked about 3–3½" (7.5–9 cm). This length depends on the overall finished length of your necklace and the number of crochet beads you plan to use. The necklace does not have a clasp, and it should be long enough to slip over your head. With another T-pin, tack this first strand to one side on your board. Begin knotting and threading the next strand, staggering the beads and knots so they're spaced in a different way than the first strand. In other words, if there's an empty space on the first strand, put a bead in the corresponding space on the second strand. When the second strand is the same length as the first strand, tack it out of the way with a T-pin. Repeat the process with 6 strands total, leaving 2 strands empty.

Step 10: Weave the 8 strands together, using a combination of loose braiding and knotting to keep the strands even. You may need to add more knots and beads on one or more strands so the lengths are all the same. Knot the 8 strands together with an overhand knot and take all 8 strands through the crochet bead. It may be easier to thread the strands on a Big Eye needle and take them through the bead center one or two at a time. Make another overhand knot on the other side of the crochet bead with all 8 strands. Using another T-pin, tack the filled bead onto the board so it's held in place. Set 7 strands aside, and begin the knotting and bead threading process again.

Step 11: Knot and bead 6 strands, then braid all 8 strands together. Make an overhand knot and thread the 8 strands through the back neck 2" (5 cm) bead crochet tube, leaving the 8 strands sticking out the other side of tube.

Step 12: Repeat the same process on the other side of the centerpiece knot, threading through the crochet beads and the back bead in the same pattern as the first side.

Step 13: Using the Big Eye needle, stitch each thread back into the tube several times to secure. You can

also stitch through the larger-holed beads a few more times for more strength.

Extra Embellishment

If your center bead tube is uneven, or too thin in places, add some extra beads. Using the 10" (25.5 cm) tail attached to the end of the center bead tube (see step 6), thread a Big Eye needle and insert it through the tube and up to the surface, adding beads as you go for more color, larger size, another shape, or whatever else you think the center bead tube needs. End this thread by bringing it out of a small bead (at least 8°) on the exterior of the tube and knotting it twice. Seal the tails with nail polish and trim close to the work.

Little Bag of Jewels

If you love trendy yarns made from natural and synthetic fibers, metallic threads, and beads, this is a great project. All you need to get started are your materials, a crochet hook, and a desire to create a unique piece of art in the guise of a simple purse. This small bag works up quickly, and it's the perfect size for credit cards, a cell phone, keys, and of course, mad money.

The bead amounts will make a 4 × 6" (10 × 15 cm) bag.

MATERIALS
- Seed Beads: 10 each, 6°, 8°, with a few 11°s
- Assorted accent beads: 5 each of Miracles, M&Ms, fiber optic, glass donuts, furnace glass, charms, 6–10mm glass beads
- Yarns: 30–50 grams of 3 or 4 yarns in different weights; fingering, sport, DK (see Yarn Resources page 122). The yarn combinations are held together and worked as one.
- 1 spool black Mastex
- 1 bobbin black Nymo F

NOTIONS
- Crochet hook, size G (4.5 mm)
- Tapestry needle for yarns
- Beading needle
- Big Eye needle
- Scissors
- Nail polish or correction fluid

GAUGE
- 16 sc = 4" (10 cm). Adjust hook size if necessary to obtain the correct gauge.

Note: Review Crochet and Beading Tips and Techniques, pages 17 and 29, before starting the project:
Flat crochet, page 23
Framing, page 30
Stringing beads, page 29

Bag Front

1 *Step 1:* Use Mastex thread and cut the end at an angle. Stiffen end with nail polish or correction fluid and let dry. You will be working directly from the spool. Using the stiffened end of Mastex, string the seed and accent beads in a random pattern. Frame a few larger accent beads with 3 or 4 seed beads on either side, and use them as a group in one st. The seed beads will allow the larger beads to hang from the bag. Use other large accent beads or charms as a single bead worked in one sc st at a time.

2 *Step 2:* Select 2 or 3 yarns and a hook size that will provide the correct gauge. Hold the yarns together and use them as a single strand. Work a few rows of crochet to make sure the yarns maintain gauge, work well together, and don't obscure the beads. When you're happy with the results, begin your purse. The purse is made in one continuous piece, then folded in half to form the front and back sections. On the front of the bag, I used large accent and seed beads and substituted 2 of the yarns for 2 others in the middle section. To make the back, I used all yarns and no beads in the crochet, and changed my yarn combination about halfway up.

3 *Step 3:* With the yarns (including the Mastex) held together as one, work as follows: **Foundation row:** (without beads) Make a slipknot, leaving about a 4" (10 cm) tail. Ch 16, ch 2 to turn.
Row 1: (without beads) Insert hook into third ch from hook and sc, *sc in next st; repeat instructions from * to end of row, ch 2 to turn.
Row 2: (with beads) Insert hook into second sc from side edge and work sc, *slip a single bead, or a group of beads, up to the hook and sc in next ch; work sc in each of next 2 chs without adding beads*; repeat instructions between * * to last ch, end row with sc.
Row 3: (without beads) Insert hook into second sc from side edge and work sc; *sc in next st; repeat instructions from * to end of row, ch 2 to turn.

Note: If you insert the bead(s) into the same st position each time, they will stack up in vertical lines, so vary their placement, unless you want a vertical stack. My beads zigzag a little because I moved over one or two sts before inserting the beads on some rows, then moved back to the original st on following rows. Remember, the beads are added on alternate rows only, so they won't end up on the wrong side of the bag. Work one row with beads, then one row without beads.

If possible, try to space the beads between the first and last sc and work the first and last sc without beads. This leaves a smooth area at each side edge that you can use for seaming the sides together. You may crochet several rows without beads if you wish, but just be sure you're on the right side of the work when you start adding beads again.

Step 4: Continue in your pattern of yarns and beads for about 4 rows. By then, you'll have an

idea how the combination looks. Pay attention to the gauge, and check the width of your purse. The sides should be straight and even. If you like what you have, continue. If not, pull out the crochet, change your yarn combinations, and begin again.

5 *Step 5:* Assuming you like what you have, continue repeating rows 2 and 3. After working 6 rows or so, drop 1 or 2 of the yarns and add 1 or 2 new yarns. Be sure to leave 4" (10 cm) tails to weave in later each time you add or drop yarns. When the front measures about 6" (15 cm) or desired length, begin the back.

Bag Back

6 *Step 6:* When you reach the halfway point, cut the Mastex thread leaving about 6"(15 cm) to weave in through the crochet sts to secure. Don't cut the yarns. Continue working rows of sc without beads and changing 1 or 2 yarns every few rows. The finished crocheted piece should be a rectangle that equals double the bag length. Keep a consistent tension throughout to increase the strength of your stitches and the overall aesthetics of the design.

7 *Step 7:* When the body of the purse is finished, whipstitch the sides together with a threaded tapestry needle (be sure to use a smooth yarn), or crochet the sides closed with sl st or sc.

Strap

8 *Step 8:* The strap is made with several strands of yarn held together as one. You can work a crochet ch, make a braid, or leave the yarns as separate strands. My strap is a crochet chain, and the finished length is about 40" (101.5 cm). Keep in mind that crocheting or braiding the strands together will strengthen the strap. Using one of the smooth yarns and a tapestry needle, stitch one end of the strap to the top of a side seam with an overhand stitch. Thread the yarn tail through several sts on the wrong side to secure. Attach the second strap end to the other side of bag in the same manner.

Surface Embellishment

When the bag is finished, you can also embellish it with more beads in random or precise patterns. Thread a beading needle with Nymo F and weave your way through the fibers adding beads, decorative buttons, or charms, and stitching them to the bag as you work. Hide the thread in the crochet sts, and knot securely at both ends. Trim the tails close to the work.

Talisman Necklace

Several years ago, while visiting my daughter in Santa Cruz, California, I found some wonderful vintage black-and-white beads that looked like Keds sneakers and playing cards. I bought a black, white, and crystal bead soup to go with them. Black and white was a new color palette for me, and it was refreshing to create with it. The Talisman Necklace features an unusual double-stranded design that invites you to explore free-form bead crochet with your own collection of meaningful, rare, or unique beads.

The bead amounts listed will make one 2 × 3½" (5 × 9 cm) crochet talisman, with a 36" (91.5 cm) neckpiece.

MATERIALS

- Seed Beads: 1 tube each, 6° and 8°
- Assorted accent beads: 10 each, triangles, squares, hexes, glass hoops, tiny hearts, small flat ovals, magatamas, 4mm–6mm Miracle, fiber optic, small flower beads, miracle rondelles, small charms
- Assorted beads for neckpiece: Furnace glass, 4 and 8mm round, 4mm Austrian crystals, rondelles, tubes, Miracle beads, 2-holed horizontal beads
- 1 spool black Mastex, or a color to complement your beads
- 1 bobbin black Nymo F

NOTIONS

- Crochet hook, size 2 (2.5 mm) steel
- Bead spinner
- Beeswax
- Nail polish or correction fluid
- T-pins for knotting
- Big Eye needles, both lengths— 2½" (6.5 cm) and 5" (12.5 cm)
- Macramé board, foamcore, cork- board, or anything you can stick pins into

GAUGE

36 sc with beads = 4" (10 cm). Adjust hook size if necessary to obtain the correct gauge.

Note: Review Crochet and Beading Tips and Techniques, pages 17 and page 29, before starting the project:
Flat crochet, page 23
Fringes, page 36

Crocheted Talisman

1 *Step 1:* Using a bead spinner or bowl, mix together a bead soup, including 6° and 8° seed beads, 4–8mm round, triangles, squares, teardrops, faceted oval Austrian crystal, glass hoops, squares, small flower beads, and other small accent beads. The beads can be a variety of colors or all from the same color family. Cut the end of a spool of Mastex thread at an angle. Stiffen the end with nail polish or correction fluid and let dry. You will be working directly from the spool.

2 *Step 2:* Using the stiffened end as a needle, string 3 yd (2.75 m) of Mastex with beads in groups of 3 or as bead soup from bead spinner. String fourteen 8° seed beads, six 8° hexes, one accent bead, six 8° hexes, four 6°s. Then string 8°s and 6°s to provide space for an accent bead to be clearly visible over the other beads. Alternate 8°s and 6°s. Make sure that the larger beads have enough space around them to hang freely on top of the lower beads. This instruction will make sense when you begin crocheting.

3 *Step 3:* Leaving a 4"(10 cm) tail of Mastex, work as follows: **Foundation row:** Ch 18, ch 2 to turn.
Row 1: (without beads) Insert hook into the third ch from the hook and work sc, *sc in next ch; repeat instructions from * to end of row, ch 2.
Row 2: (with beads) Slide 3 beads up to the hook, work sc in the second sc from the side edge, *slide 3 beads up to the hook and work sc in next sc; repeat instructions from * to end of row, ch 2.
Row 3: (without beads) Insert hook into the second sc from the side edge and work sc; *sc in next sc; repeat instructions from * to end of row.

Repeat rows 2 and 3, alternating one row with beads, one row without, until the piece measures about 3½" (9 cm) long, or desired size.

Branched Fringes

4 *Step 4:* Cut 24" (61 cm) of Nymo F and thread a Big Eye needle, fold thread in half to double, and wax well. Make an overhand knot at the thread ends and stitch into the wrong side of the bead crochet so the knot is hidden. String on a "stem" of seventeen 8°s, pull thread through the last bead, skip that bead, then pass back through 5 beads. *First branch:* Pick up six more 8°s, push them down to the same length as the original stem, then skip the bottom bead and pass back through 5 beads to the original stem. Pass back through 2 beads of the original stem. *Second branch:* pick up 5 more 8°s and pull down the stem. Skip the bottom bead and pass back through 4 beads, then pass back through 2 beads on the stem. *Third branch:* Pick up 4 more beads, pull down the stem, skip the bottom bead, and pass back through 3 beads, and then pass back through the remaining stitches on the main stem. Stitch the fringe into the lower edge of the crocheted piece. Move over 1 stitch along the lower edge of the crocheted piece and begin another fringe. Intersperse branch fringes with single fringe strands or fringe loops for variety.

Necklace Strap

5 *Step 5:* Cut 2 strands of Mastex, each 48" (122 cm) long. These are an appropriate length to complete the 36" (91.5 cm) necklace strap, plus 12" (30.5 cm) extra to use when crocheting the finished strap to the talisman piece. If you plan to change the necklace length, remember to include the extra 12" (30.5 cm) to join the necklace strap and talisman together. Cut both strand ends at an angle and stiffen with nail polish or correction fluid. Tie 2 ends into one top corner of your crocheted piece, leaving a 6" (15 cm) tail. With T-pins, tack the crocheted base onto the macramé, or foamcore board, to hold it in place, as you plan your straps.

6 *Step 6:* Lay out an approximation of your strap design, for an idea of spacing and length. Begin stringing the beads, 6°s, 8°s, and your other necklace beads onto the necklace thread. If you're using 2-holed horizontal beads, be sure to keep them parallel with each other, and keep the spacing on both sides of necklace even, otherwise the necklace and talisman will not hang straight. You will be working the strap length from one front end, around the neck to the other front end. Both front ends of the strap are then crocheted into the top edge of the talisman piece using the 12" (30.5 cm) thread tails reserved for this. After crocheting the pieces together, stitch the strap ends in place with doubled Nymo F to secure. Trim the tails close to the work. Wear this piece with enthusiasm and hope.

Sunrise Brooch

As the rays of the rising sun slowly spread like ripples on a pond, this brooch glows with waves of color that move out from its center. Experience a rebirth in your life as you create this mesmerizing bauble. Follow the ancient spiral motif that reflects the death of old patterns or ideas and the inevitable dawn of new ones that take you to points unknown. Here you will explore circular bead crochet in brilliant colors around a striking dichroic cabochon embellished with seed beads as the luminous focal point.

The bead amounts will make one brooch, about 2½"(6.5 cm) in diameter.

MATERIALS

- Seed Beads: ½ small tube each, 8°s, 11°s, and 15°s in your choice of colors
- Cabochon: 1" × 1½" (2.5 × 3.8 cm), dichroic or fused glass or semiprecious stone
- Yarn: 50 yards of fingering or sportweight yarn in colors to complement your beads. (see Yarn Resources, page 122)
- 1 spool Gudebrod F
- 1 bobbin Nymo F
- Pin back: 1½" (3.8 cm) long

NOTIONS

- Crochet hook, size 2 (2.5 mm) steel
- Beeswax
- Big Eye needle
- Beading needles
- Scissors
- Stitch marker
- Nail polish or correction fluid
- Superglue (optional)

GAUGE

- 40 sc with beads = 4" (10 cm). Adjust hook size if necessary to obtain the correct gauge.

Note: Review Crochet and Beading Tips and Techniques, pages 17 and 29, before starting the project:

Crochet, circular flat, page 24

Flat (one-drop) peyote st, page 32

Peyote stitch decreases, page 34

Cabochon Base

1 *Step 1:* Cut the end of a spool of Gudebrod F thread at an angle. Stiffen the end with nail polish or correction fluid and let dry. You will be working directly from the spool. Using the stiffened end as your needle, string 12" (30.5 cm) of 8° seed beads. The crochet base under the cabochon is made without beads to create a flat surface, so set the strung beads aside until you've finished that section of the base.

2 *Step 2:* Work as follows:

Foundation Row: (without beads) With yarn only, ch 4, join into circle with sl st. Ch 2 (counts as one st). From this point, the base is made with continuous rnds, without turns or joins.

Rnd 1: (without beads) Work 7 sc into the circle—8 sts. Place stitch marker on turning ch to indicate beg of rnd; move up with each new rnd.

Rnd 2: (without beads) Work 2 sc in each st to end of rnd, move marker—16 sts.

Rnd 3: (without beads) *Work 1 sc in first sc, 2 sc in next sc*; repeat instructions between * * to end of rnd, move marker—24 sts.

Rnd 4: (without beads) *Work 2 sc in first sc, 1 sc in next sc*; repeat instructions between * * to end of rnd—36 sts.

Repeat rnds 2 through 4 until the circle is slightly larger than your cabochon. The number of increases made and number of rows worked will depend on your gauge and the required size of the base. If the circle edges begin to curl up, work more increases on rows 3 or 4. If the edges start to ruffle, work fewer increases. I've used an oval cab, 1½" (3.8 cm) long and ¾" (2 cm) wide, so my nonbead section measures 1¾" (5.5 cm) in diameter.

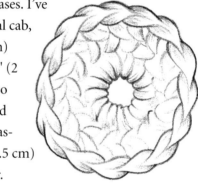

3 *Step 3:* When the nonbeaded base for the cabochon is the desired size, leave a 6" (15 m) tail and join the stranded Gudebrod thread. Hold it together with the yarn and work as one. Work each rnd with beads.

First bead rnd: (without increases) Slide your beads up to the hook and use one bead per st to work sc in each st to end of rnd.

Next bead rnd: (with increases) Work 2 sc with beads in each sc of previous rnd.

Repeat last 2 rnds until brooch is desired size. My brooch measures 2½" (6.5 cm) in diameter. The outer edges should be slightly scalloped or curved to add to the floral-like shape. To make ruffled edges, work another rnd of sc without beads and embellish further by stitching a strand of beads around the outer edge; attach the strand between sc sts and unattached over the top of each sc. I used Nymo F with seed beads around the edges of my brooch.

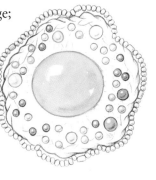

4 *Step 4:* When the base is finished, place your cabochon in the center of the nonbeaded section of the base. If you prefer, put a drop of superglue on the bottom to help anchor the cabochon. Allow the glue to set before you continue.

Encase the Cabochon

5 *Step 5:* Cut 2 yd (1.82 m) of Nymo F and thread on beading needle. Wax the thread well. Tie a knot at one end, insert the needle from the wrong side of the work upward, then pull the thread through to the right side of the work. String on four 8º seed beads, needle down to the wrong side of the work, and then backstitch past the last 2 seed beads just added. As you work, insert the backstitches in the crochet base to hide them.

Needle up between the 4 seed beads (2 seed beads on each side of the needle), draw the thread through to the right side of the work and pass back through the last 2 beads added. *With needle and thread on the right side of the work, string on 2 more 8° seed beads, needle down to the wrong side of the work and backstitch past the 2 new beads. Needle up at the beginning of the 2 new beads and pass back through both beads to anchor*. Repeat instructions between * *, adding two 8° beads for each stitch until you have completed a circle of beads around the cab. With Nymo thread only (no beads), pass back through all the seed beads once again to pull them together and strengthen the piece.

6 *Step 6:* Continue to encase the cabochon, using peyote st for this section, as follows:

Row 1: Using Nymo F, a beading needle, and 8º seed beads, work one-drop peyote above the first row of beads.

Row 2: Work one-drop peyote with 11º seed beads, pulling the thread tight, and decreasing as necessary to enclose the cab securely. Work a third row of one-drop peyote with 11º seed beads, if necessary, to enclose the cab securely.

EMBELLISHING THE CABOCHON

Step 7: With the same thread (or join a new thread if necessary), *strand six 15ºs, one 8º, six 15˚s, and stretch the strand across the cab face at an angle, connecting into the top row of peyote worked with 11˚ beads. Pass back through the 11˚ bead to the right side of the work*. Repeat instructions between * * as necessary, weaving your way back and forth across the cab face to create an open, lacy grid. On the wrong side of the work, weave remaining thread through several crochet sts to secure. Trim the tail close to the work.

Attach Pin Back

Step 8: With a double strand of Nymo F threaded on a beading needle, stitch the pin back in place

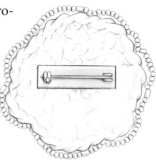

to the wrong side of the crocheted piece and whipstitch firmly to attach. Weave the thread through several crochet sts to secure, then trim the tail close to the work. If you wish to hide the whipstitching and cover the base of the pin back, make a small peyote rectangle and stitch it over the center section to the crocheted background.

Finishing

Step 9: With a Big Eye needle, weave any loose yarn tails through several crochet sts on the wrong side the work to secure. With a beading needle, weave loose threads back and forth through several beads to secure, tie knot, and trim the tails close to the work.

Crimson Concentric Circles Purse

This bold design of interlocking circles is a tour de force of circular, triangular, and free-form bead crochet. The beads, color, and texture combine to create a striking ornamental evening bag complemented by beaded embellishment and a braided strap of three beaded chains. Wend your way around the curving maze, explore the variety of circular patterns, and create some patterns of your own!

The bead amounts will make one purse about 6" (15 cm) in diameter.

MATERIALS

- Seed Beads: Eight 6" (15 cm) tubes of 8°, six 6" (15 cm) tubes of 11°, four 6" (15 cm) tubes of 6°
- Assorted Accent Beads: Thirty 8mm crackle beads, 30 red-and-gold barrels, 1 strand Miracle tubes, 100 M&Ms, 60 tiny teardrops, 40 gold vermeil spacers and twisted circles, 1 strand 6mm Miracle beads, 50 bronze glass donuts, 40 matte rondelles, 1 hologram bead with gold and silver flecks on black onyx. 1 square dichroic glass bead (a Sara Creekmore bead is shown in the photo)
- Yarns: 50 grams of 3 or 4 designer yarns held together as one. You may choose any combination of yarns that will give you the gauge. (see Yarn Resources, page 122)
- 1 spool each of rose and scarlet Mastex thread
- 1 spool each of lavender and Yale blue bonded polyester thread
- 1 spool gold metallic YLI thread
- 1 bobbin black Nymo F
- 1 purchased purple satin ribbon flower, ½" (1.3 cm) diameter (available from craft stores)
- 1 Red pressed glass rose button, about ½" (1.3 cm) diameter

NOTIONS

▥ 2 crochet hooks, size 5 (1.7 mm) steel for bead crochet; size G (4.25 mm) for yarn

▥ Size 10 beading needle

▥ Beeswax

▥ Big Eye needle

▥ Measuring tape

▥ Scissors

▥ Stitch markers

▥ Nail polish or correction fluid

GAUGE FOR YARNS

16 sc = 4" (10 cm)

Note: Review Crochet Tips and Techniques, page 17 before starting project:

Flat crochet, page 23

Circular Flat crochet, page 24

Purse Front

The front of the purse is composed of 8 circles, fitted together with additional triangular or freeform pieces of bead crochet that are embellished and whipstitched together. Each circle is made separately, worked in continuous rounds without joining or turning. (See photo on page 105 for individual circle markers.)

CIRCLE A—CENTERPIECE. ABOUT 2¼" (5.5 CM) DIAMETER

① *Step 1:* Using scarlet Mastex thread and working directly from the spool, thread a Big Eye needle. You can also cut the end of the Mastex at an angle, stiffen it with nail polish or correction fluid, and use the stiffened end as a needle. String the *first*

beading pattern as follows: *2 bright red Aurora Borealis (AB) 8°s, 1 red-and-gold barrel, 2 bright red AB 8°s, 5 clear red 8°s, 1 dark bronze donut, 2 red AB 8°s, 1 barrel, 2 red AB 8°s, 5 red 8°s, 1 donut; repeat stringing sequence from * until you have a total of 15 barrels and 15 donuts, then end with 5 red 8°s.

② *Step 2:* Continuing with the same thread, string *beading pattern #2:* string 3 red Aurora Borealis (AB) opaque 11°s, 1 clear red faceted crystal rondelle, 3 (AB) opaque 11°s, *three 11°s, 1 clear red faceted crystal rondelle, six 11°s; repeat from * until you have 15 clear red faceted crystal rondelles spaced on your string. *Beading pattern #3:* String 16 red 6°s.

③ *Step 3:* With crochet hook and same Mastex thread, work ***Foundation Row*** as follows: Ch 4, join into a circle with sl st. Add a stitch marker to indicate the beginning of the rnd, and move marker up with each new rnd.

Rnd 1: (increases) Work 2 sc in each foundation st, join with slip st—8 sts.

Rnd 2: Work 2 sc in each st to end of rnd—16 sts.

Rnd 3: Slide beads up to the hook and sc using one 6º bead in each stitch.

Rnd 4: Slide beads up to the hook and *sc using a cluster of three 11ºs, 1 crystal, three 11ºs in each stitch*; repeat instructions between * * to end of rnd.

Rnd 5: (increases) Without beads, work 2 sc in each st. *Note:* Too many increases will make the edges ruffle. If this happens, pull out the crochet and work the rnd again with fewer increases.

Rnd 6: Slide beads up to the hook and sc with 8°s, barrels, and donuts, alternating sc sts with and without beads as needed to keep the edges flat.

Rnd 7: (increases) Sc without beads, increasing 2 sc in 1 sc as needed to maintain even edges.

The circle should be about 2¼" (5.5 cm) in diameter after rnd 7. If the circle is smaller, add another rnd without beads.

4 *Step 4:* With Nymo F threaded on beading needle, attach the dichroic red square bead in the center space. Cut thread leaving a 4" (10 cm) to weave in later.

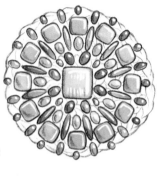

CIRCLE B—ABOUT 2" (5 CM) IN DIAMETER

1 *Step 1:* With Yale blue bonded polyester thread, and working directly from the spool, thread a Big Eye needle, or work with the stiffened end of thread as your needle (see Circle A). String four beading patterns as follows. *Beading pattern #1:* string 8 sections of 8°s in 4 colors: 8 magenta, 8 matte red, 8 blue, 8 shiny red AB (32 beads total). Continue with the same thread and string *beading pattern #2:* *String one 8°, 1 rondelle, two 8°s, one 6mm, two 8°s, 1 faceted rondelle, two 8°s, 1 faceted 6mm oval, two 8°s, 1 Miracle tube, one 8°; repeat beading sequence from * once more,

ending with one 8°. Continue with the same thread and string *beading pattern #3:* String thirty 8° red hexes. Then string *beading pattern #4:* one 8°, 2 twisted tiny gold vermeil rings, one 8° hex, one 8mm red crackle bead, one 8° hex, 2 twisted tiny gold vermeil rings, one 8°.

2 *Step 2:* Continue with the Yale blue bonded polyester thread and work **Foundation row:** Ch 4, join into a circle with sl st. Add a stitch marker to indicate the beginning of the rnd, and move marker up with each new rnd.

Rnd 1: (increases) Work 2 sc in each foundation stitch—8 sts.

Rnd 2: Sc in each st to last st, then slide beads up to the hook and sc with the last 4 beads in beading pattern #4.

Rnd 3: (increases) Work 2 sc in each st to end of rnd.

Note: Increase more frequently if the edges begin to curl upward, less frequently if the edges begin to ruffle.

Rnd 4: (with beads) Slide 2 hex beads up to the hook, sc using 2 beads in each st to end of rnd. Increase as needed.

Rnd 5: (with beads) Slide a cluster of 3 beads up to the hook, sc 3 beads into each st to end of rnd.

Rnd 6: (without beads) Work 2 sc in each st to end of rnd.

Rnd 7: (with beads) Slide beads up to the hook, sc groups of 3 beads in each st to end of rnd. If you have a few stranded beads remaining, continue to use them in the next rnd.

Rnds 8 and 9: Sc without beads, increasing as needed to maintain even edges, until the circle measures the desired diameter—about 2" (5 cm). Cut thread leaving a 4" (10 cm) tail to weave in later.

CIRCLE C—ABOUT 2" (5 CM) IN DIAMETER

Step 1: With rose Mastex thread, and working directly from the spool, thread a Big Eye needle, or use stiffened end of thread (see Circle A). String two beading patterns as follows. *Pattern #1:* string a random pattern of beads, which may include *one 8°, one M&M, two 8°s, one 6mm, two 8°s, 1 oval 6mm faceted crystal, one 8°, one dark red glass flower, one 8°, one Miracle tube, one 8°, 1 vintage pink oval bead*; repeat your beading sequence between * * until there are 14–16 accent beads. *Note:* You can experiment with the different sizes and shapes—just be sure the string has 14—16 accent beads total. Continue with the same thread and string *Pattern #2:* string forty-four 8°s.

Step 2: Continuing with rose Mastex thread, work **Foundation row:** Ch 4, join into a circle with sl st. Add a stitch marker to indicate the beginning of the rnd, and move marker up with each new rnd.

Rnds 1 and 2: (increases) Work 2 sc in each st—16 sts.

Rnd 3: (with beads) Slide beads up to the hook and work in sc using random beads; increase as needed to maintain flat edges.

Following rnds: When you've finished the random beads, cont *sc in rnds using two 8°s in each st; repeat instructions from * until work measures about 1½" (3.8 cm) in diameter. Cut rose Mastex thread leaving a 4" (10 cm) tail, and join lavender Mastex thread.

Next 3 rnds: (without beads) With lavender thread, work sc, and cont to increase where necessary. The finished circle should measure 2" (5 cm) in diameter or desired size. Cut thread leaving a 4" (10 cm) tail to weave in later.

CIRCLE D—ABOUT 1¼" (4.5 CM) IN DIAMETER

Step 1: With Yale blue bonded polyester thread, and working directly from the spool, thread a Big Eye needle, or use stiffened end of thread (see Circle A). String the following *beading patterns:* twelve 11°s; three 8°s in 2 colors (1 red AB, 1 red-violet S/L, 1 red AB) 5 times; fifteen 11°s; three 8°s in 2 colors (1 red AB, 1 red-violet S/L, 1 red AB) 12 times.

Step 2: Continuing with Yale blue bonded polyester thread, work **Foundation row:** Ch 4, join into a circle with sl st. Add a stitch marker to indicate the beginning of the rnd and move marker up with each new rnd.

Rnds 1 and 2: Sc in each st to end of rnd, increasing as needed to maintain flat edges.

Rnd 3: (with beads) Slide beads up to hook, sc three 11°s in each of next 4 sts, then sc three 8°s in each stitch to end of rnd.

Rnd 4: Repeat Rnd 3 using all 11°s, increasing as needed to maintain flat edges.

Rnd 5: Holding twelve 8° aside until rnd 7, repeat rnd 3 using 8°s.

Rnd 6: (without beads) Sc, increasing as needed.

Rnd 7: (with beads) Sc, adding remaining twelve 8°s randomly to end of rnd.

After rnd 7, circle should be about 1¼" (4.5 cm) in diameter.

Step 3: With Nymo F threaded on beading needle, attach the red matte star-studded plastic oval bead in the center of the circle, framed with an 8° and a gold vermeil ring on each side. Cut both threads leaving 4" (10 cm) tails to weave in later.

CIRCLE E—ABOUT 2" (5 CM) IN DIAMETER

Step 1: With rose Mastex thread, working directly from the spool, thread a Big Eye needle, or use stiffened end of thread (see Circle A). String the following patterns: 9½"(24 cm) red hex beads—this will use about one 3½" (9 cm) tube. *Two red 8°s, one 6mm Miracle, two 8°s, 1 Miracle tube, two 8°s, one 6mm faceted crystal, two 8°s, 1 Miracle tube, two 8°s; repeat from * ending with a total of five 6mm Miracle beads, 7 Miracle tubes, and 3 faceted crystals. String three 11°s in 3 different colors (peach, red, shocking pink) 16 times.

Step 2: Continuing with rose Mastex thread, work **Foundation row:** Ch 4, join into a circle with sl st.

Add a stitch marker to indicate the beginning of the rnd, and move marker up with each new rnd.

Rnds 1–6: (without beads) Sc to end of rnd increasing as needed to maintain flat edges. Work should measure about ⅝" (1.5 cm) from center.

Rnds 7 and 8: (with beads) Slide beads up to the hook and *sc next st with three 11°s, without beads sc in next 3 sts*; repeat instructions between * * working around the circle in the same patt until all 11°s are used. Increase sts as needed. It's not a problem if beads overlap or if you need to work another rnd to finish beads.

Next rnd: (with beads) Slide beads up to the hook and *sc with a cluster of beads (one 8°, one 6mm Miracle, one 8/0), then skip 1–2 stitches (to equal the bead-cluster length), sc in next st; rep from * around until the bead clusters are finished.

Next rnd: (with beads) *Sc with 3 hexes, sc in next st without beads, sc with 4 hexes*; repeat instructions between * * alternating sc without beads and sc with 3 or 4 beads until all beads are finished.

Next rnds: Continue working sc without beads, increasing stitches as needed to prevent the outer edges from curling up. Finish when circle measures about 2" (5 cm) in diameter, or desired size.

Step 3: With Nymo F threaded on sewing or beading needle, attach purple ribbon flower in center of circle. Cut both threads leaving 4" (10 cm) tails to weave in later.

CIRCLE F—ABOUT 2½" (6.5 CM)

Step 1: With lavender bonded polyester thread, working directly from the spool, thread a Big Eye needle, or use stiffened end of thread (see Circle A). String the following patterns: 5" (12.5 cm) of red AB 8°s (about ½ of 6" [15 cm] tube). String 11" (28 cm) in groups of one red AB 8°, 1 S/L red-violet 8°, 1 red AB 8°. String 1 matte red AB rondelle, one 8mm blue-green crackle bead, and 1 matte red AB rondelle as a group 10 times, end pattern with ten 8mm beads total. String 1 red and 1 black color-lined 6° 20 times.

Step 2: Continuing with the lavender thread, work **Foundation row:** Ch 4, join into a circle with sl st. Add a stitch marker to indicate the beginning of the rnd, and move marker up with each new rnd.
Rnds 1–5: (without beads) Work in sc, increasing by working 2 sc in 1 sc as needed to maintain flat even edges.
Rnd 6: (with beads) Sc with three 8°s, *sc without beads in next st, sc with 8°s in next st*; repeat instructions between * * to end of rnd. Increase as needed to maintain flat edges.
Rnd 7: (with beads) *Sc with three 8°s, sc in next st, sc with 3 beads; repeat from * to end of rnd.
Rnd 8: Repeat rnd 7. Finished circle should measure about 2½" (6.5 cm). If necessary, work more rnds without beads until circle is correct size, and making increases as needed to maintain even edges. Cut thread leaving a 4" (10 cm) tail.

Step 3: With Nymo F threaded on beading needle, and well waxed, stitch the center hole of the red pressed glass rose button into the center of the crochet circle. String one 4mm blue faceted crystal bead, a gold vermeil ring, and 1 red 11° seed bead on top of the rose button, then skip the 11° and pass back through the ring, crystal bead, and button, and stitch into the wrong side of the crochet sts. Repeat threading once more through the same 4 beads for strength, then anchor with a few sts into the crochet base. Cut both threads leaving 4" (10 cm) tails to weave in later.

CIRCLE G—ABOUT 2" (5 CM) IN DIAMETER

Step 1: With red Mastex thread, working directly from the spool, thread a Big Eye needle, or use stiffened end of thread (see Circle A). String the following patterns: 17" (43 cm) of bright red AB 8°s. String *1 clear red 8°, 1 tiny amber teardrop, one 8°, 1 gold vermeil spacer, 1 garnet M&M, 1 gold vermeil spacer, 1 red 8°, 1 teardrop; repeat from * until there are a total of 16 teardrops and 16 M&Ms on the string.

Step 2: Continuing with red Mastex thread, work **Foundation row:** Ch 4, join into a circle with sl st. Add a stitch marker to indicate the beginning of the rnd, and move marker up with each new rnd

Rnds 1 and 2: (without beads) Sc in each st, increase as needed.

All other rnds: Sc with bead patterns until circle is desired size, increase as needed to maintain even edges.

3 *Step 3:* With Nymo F threaded on beading needle, attach gold hologram bead in center space. Cut both threads leaving 4" (10 cm) tails to weave in later.

H and I—Small Fill-In Circles

H- about 1½" (3.8 cm) in diameter

1 *Step 1:* With red Mastex thread, working directly from the spool, thread a Big Eye needle, or use stiffened end of thread (see Circle A). String forty-eight 8°s.

2 *Step 2:* With red Mastex and gold YLI thread held together as one, work **Foundation row:** Ch 4, join into a circle with sl st.

Rnds 1 and 2: With both threads held together as one, sc to end of rnd increasing as needed to maintain even edges.

Next rnds: Continue working in rnds of sc with both threads, and begin adding groups of 3 or 4 beads, working outward until fill-in circle is desired size. Cut both threads leaving 4" (10 cm) tails to weave in later.

Circle I—about 1½" (3.8 cm) in diameter

1 *Step 1:* With lavender bonded polyester thread, working directly from the spool, thread a Big Eye

needle, or use stiffened end of thread (see Circle A). String 2½" (6.5 cm) in a random assortment of 11°s, gold vermeil twisted rings, and 8°s.

 Step 2: With lavender thread, and gold YLI thread held together as one, work **Foundation row:** Ch 4, join into a circle with sl st.

Rnds 1 and 2: With both threads held together as one, sc to end of rnd, increasing as needed.

Next rnds: Cont working in sc rnds with both yarns held together, adding groups of 3 or 4 beads and increasing as needed until circle is desired size. Cut both threads leaving 4" (10 cm) tails.

Weave in all loose tails to wrong side of circles and secure.

Circle Layout

Plan the purse design by placing the circles where you want them. See how they fit together and begin stitching with a Big Eye needle or crocheting the pieces together. I stitched in some places and crocheted in others, sometimes changing the color of thread if the spirit moved me. When you have the general shape and design worked out, you'll know where to place the fan-shaped pieces to fill the empty spaces along the edges

Fan-Shaped Pieces

Fan-shaped pieces are used to fill in empty spaces. Their sizes will vary, so consider that aspect during construction, and check the fit as you work.

The fans are worked in flat, back-and-forth crochet, and not in circles like the previous pieces.

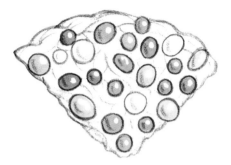

Step 1: Using your choice of thread and color, string 3" (7.5 cm) in a random pattern with 8˚s. This amount is probably more than is needed, but it's better to have too many than too few.

Step 2: Continuing with the same spool of thread, work **Foundation row:** Ch 3, ch 1 to turn.

Row 1: Insert hook in second ch from hook, work 2 sc into each foundation ch. Ch 1, turn work.

Row 2: (with beads) Slide one 8˚ bead up to hook and sc into first sc from side edge, sc with 8˚ into next stitch, sc two 8˚s into next stitch. You are now randomly choosing the number of 8˚s to use. Increase stitches as needed to obtain the width that will fill the space. Ch 1 at row end and turn work.

Row 3: (without beads) Sc in each st, increasing as needed to fill space. Ch 1, turn work. When working flat bead crochet, alternate rows with and without beads, so the beads are all located on the right side of the piece.

Row 4: (with beads) *Slide beads up to the hook and sc with 1 bead, sc next st without beads, sc next st with 2 beads, sc next st without beads, sc next st with 1 bead; repeat from * to end of row. It's not a problem if the row ends without a full repeat, the last repeat will depend on the number of increases made on earlier rows. Ch 1, turn work.

Next row: (without beads) Sc to end of row, increasing as needed. Ch 1, turn work.

Next row: (with beads) Slide beads up to the hook and sc with beads the same as previous bead rows. If the fan is large enough to complete the purse, cut yarn and thread through last st. If not, Ch 1, turn work, and continue working in the same manner, increasing on nonbead rows and working random pattern on bead rows.

When you're finished, weave in all tails to wrong side of work and secure.

Make as many fan shapes as needed for your purse.

Purse Front Construction

Stitch the fans into the empty spaces and check the overall space and place-ment. I wanted the outer edges curved, so I added extra crochet, some embellishment, and fan shapes to create the curve.

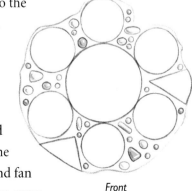

Front

I left the top opening slightly scalloped. You can embellish on top of the connecting ridges, or any place else. Make your purse as unique as you are.

Purse back

I made the back using 4 different strands of designer yarns held together as one, and chose complementary colors to go with the beads. The crochet circle construction is worked in one continuous spiral, but without beads crocheted into the stitches. If desired, beads can be added later, to embellish.

Back

1 *Step 1:* Using the larger size crochet hook, and your chosen yarns held together as one, work **Foundation row:** Ch 4, join into a circle with sl st. Add stitch marker to indicate beginning of rnd, and move up with each new rnd.

Following rnds: Work in circles of sc, increasing where necessary, until you have the desired size for the purse back. Use your discretion about where to increase and how frequently; 1 increase every other 2 or 3 stitches worked for my purse. If the edges of your purse begin to ruffle, you have too many increases. Remove the stitches back to the point where the edges are smooth, and start again using fewer increases. The number of rnds to work will depend on the gauge with your chosen yarns and the finished size of your purse.

2 *Step 2:* If you want to embellish the back, stitch on a few random beads or make a pattern and stitch the beads in place. Weave in all loose tails to wrong side of work and secure. Using a Big Eye needle and well-waxed Nymo F thread, whipstitch both Front and Back sections together around the edges; leave a 6" (15 cm) opening for the purse top.

Strap

The purse strap is made with 3 separate sections of chain bead crochet, each composed of 3 strands of fiber. Use Mastex thread in your choice of color, YLI metallic gold thread, and one of the designer yarns used in the purse back.

1 *Step 1:* Using a random assortment of leftover beads and beading needle threaded with Mastex, string 15" (38 cm) of 8˚s, hexes, triangles, an occasional 6˚, M&Ms, magatamas, and cubes.

2 *Step 2:* Using your larger crochet hook, with 3 strands of fiber held together as one, and with 3 beads in each ch st, make a chain 1½ times the desired finished strap length. Cut the tails and thread through last st to secure. Make 2 more chains the same way. Knot the ends of all 3 chains together with an overhand knot, about ½" (1.3 cm) from the ends and begin braiding them to the desired strap length.

My finished strap length, after braiding and attaching to the purse sides, measured 48" (122 cm). I also allowed an extra 2½" (6.5 cm) on each side to stitch the ends inside the purse.

When finished, stitch the strap inside the purse at each side seam, making sure that the strap is flat and untwisted.

Weave in all loose tails to wrong side to secure. Add extra embellishment, beads, or yarns if desired, and then—ENJOY!

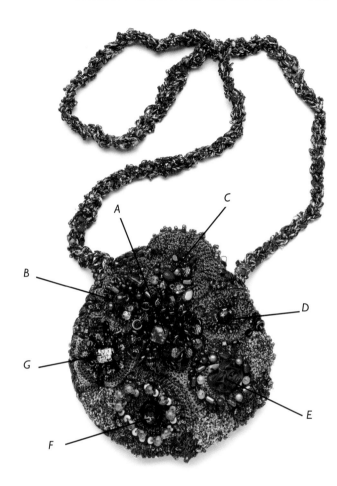

Gallery of Bead Crochet

Susannah Baker
Bracelets
8" L

Judith Bertoglio-Giffin
Rope
18" L

Judith Bertoglio-Giffin
Fringed rope
58" L

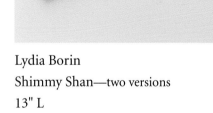

Lydia Borin
Shimmy Shan—two versions
13" L

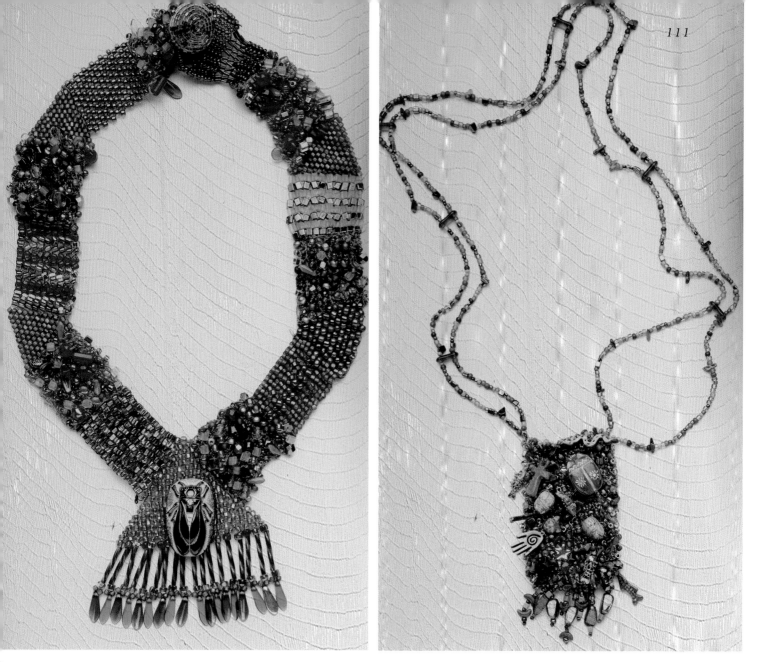

Judy Donovan
Patchwork Beaded Collar 13" L
Talisman Necklace 22" L 2" W

Martha Forsyth
Slip-stitch bead crochet ropes
Left: 11½" L
Right: 14½" L

Pat Iverson
Balkan Amulet Necklace
16½" L with fringe
4½" W

Ramona Lee
Left: Bag, 12" L with strap
Below: Miser's purse, 12" L

Dallas Lovett and Laurel Kubby
Lariat necklace with pearls
39" L

Dallas Lovett and Laurel Kubby
Necklace with bead crochet rope, pearls, and wirework
12" L

Bethany Barry
Patchwork Crocheted Scarf with bead embellishment and fringe
56" L

Kimberly Swenson
Talisman Necklace
with Macramé
Neckpiece
24" L

Bethany Barry
Necklet
11½" L

Bethany Barry
Goddess of Beads
7"

Bethany Barry
Bewitched and Bewoven Bijouterie
13" L

Acknowledgments

Writing this book has been an extraordinary process, and I could not possibly have done it alone. There are many people who have contributed much along the way, but the ones who have really made it possible are my students. Without you, I would not be able to do what I do, and live a life I love. You have helped me to find and express myself, and to grow enormously through your support, sharing, enthusiasm, creativity, humor, generosity, patience with my frequently inaccurate instructions, willingness to take my classes under many circumstances and staunch commitment to your own exploration and growth.

Thank you!

To the New Jersey/Pennsylvania students: the inimitable three Judys: Judy Donovan, Judy Gross, and Judy Demby, Sherry London, Kimberly Swenson, Arden Mosley, Susan Gibbs, Victoria Harding, Jane Causgrove, Nancy Mullins, Karen Chigounis, Marguerite Thompson, and others. To the Vermont students: Barbara Papandrea, Betty Boudreau, Nancy Spaulding, Susannah Baker, Michelle Trudeau, and others elsewhere. To the writers in my family: my mother, Alice Barry; my sister, Roxana Robinson; my brother, David Barry; and others past and present.

To NanC Meinhardt, Jeannette Cook, Cynthia Rutledge, Diane Fitzgerald, whose classes, books, insight, and friendship have both inspired me and urged me on further.

To my daughter, Kate King, who has absolutely no interest in beading, but has always believed in me.

To my husband, Andy, who has been an engineer-like rock to me through this and many other journeys in our life together. He makes me laugh and keeps me focused.

To Lydia Borin, Carol Perrenoud, and Amy Oxford for their generosity, humor, and unqualified support.

To Basil and Lucy, the studio rabbits, who offer silent companionship, soft and strokeable fur, and who provide comic relief with their bunner antics.

And last, but perhaps most important of all, to the wonderful people at Interweave Press: Jean Campbell, Betsy Armstrong, Jean Lampe, Lorrie LeJeune, Sara Boore, and Nancy Arndt. Thank you for your vision and belief in this book, your gracious and invaluable guidance, and your diplomacy and humor. You were all a gift.

And finally, to beads, without which I cannot imagine my life. Thank God for their ongoing presence and inspiration!

Bead Resources

Check with your local bead store(s) first when looking for supplies—it's important for us to support each other in the bead world! Here are some other great suppliers of a variety of things: beads, tools, threads, yarns, wire, dichroic glass, Balinese silver, and more.

Beadcats
PO Box 2840
Wilsonville, OR 97070
(503) 625-2323
www.beadcats.com
Seed beads, thread, beading supplies

Bead Cellar
6305 Westfield Ave.
Pennsauken, NJ 08035
(856) 665-4744
www.beadcellar.com
Seed beads, beading supplies, books

Beadwrangler/Lydia Borin
228 Sun Ct. N.
Tampa, FL 33613
(800) 235-0375
www.beadwrangler.com
Threads, tools, books, designs

Bethany Barry at Beads by the Lake
PO Box 188
Forest Dale, VT 05745
(802) 247-4610
www.bethanybarry.com
Mastex and Nymo F threads, beads, and Original Design Kits

Caravan Beads, Inc.
915 Forest Ave.
Portland ME 04103
(207) 761-2503
www.caravanbeads.com
Seed beads, Delicas, and more

Fire Mountain Gems
One Fire Mountain Way
Grants Pass, OR 97526
(800) 355-2137
www.firemountaingems.com
Seed beads, glass beads, metal beads, findings

Lacis
2982 Adeline St.
Berkeley, CA 94703
(510) 843-7178
www.lacis.com
Crochet hooks, tools, ribbons, embroidery supplies

Shipwreck Beads
8560 Commerce Place Dr.
NE Lacey, WA 98516
(360) 754-2323
www.shipwreckbeads.com
Seed, glass, and metal beads, tools

Singaraja Imports
94 Main St.
Vineyard Haven, MA 02568
(800) 865-8856
www.singarajaimports.com
Balinese silver

Soft Flex Products
PO Box 80
Sonoma, CA 95476
(707) 938-3539
www.softflexcompany.com
Soft Flex, Artistic Wire, beads

Studio Sararuna
Division of Sara Creekmore Glass, Inc.
PO Box 1106
Magdalena, NM 87825
(505) 854-2912
www.sararuna.com
Dichroic glass beads

Yarn Resources

Here are just a few of the yarns that can be used for the projects in this book. In general, don't be afraid to experiment with yarns that you like, though be aware that fuzzy yarns such as mohair or angora will probably hide your beads. As long as you get the gauge specified in the pattern instructions you may use any combination of yarns. Unless you decide to change the pattern dramatically, or make a larger piece, you'll only need one ball or skein of each different yarn to make the yarn-based items in this book.

Most of these yarns are available at your local yarn shop or from an online shop such as Woodland Woolworks (www.woodlandwoolworks.com) or Patternworks (www.patternworks.com), but please check with your local yarn shop first when you're looking for supplies.

Berroco
PO Box 367
14 Elmdale Rd.
Uxbridge, MA 01569-0367
www.berroco.com
Mosaic FX, ladder-type novelty (100% nylon; 78 yd (72 m): 25g)

Brown Sheep Co.
100662 Cty. Rd. 16
Mitchell, NE 69357
(308) 635-2198
www.brownsheep.com
Wildfoote, sportweight sock (75% wool, 25% nylon; 215 yd [197 m]/50 g)

Classic Elite Yarns, Inc.
300 Jackson St.
Lowell, MA 01852
Fame, worsted-weight (25% silk, 75% rayon; 116 yd [106 m]/50 g)

Knitting Fever, Inc. (KFI)
35 Debevoise Ave.
Roosevelt, NY 11575
(516) 546-3600
www.knittingfever.com
Flutter, eyelash novelty (100% polyester; 75 yd [69 m]/ 20g)

Koigu
RR#1
Williamsford, ON
Canada N0H 2V0
(800) 765-WOOL
www.koigu.com
Painter's Palette, sportweight (100% merino wool; 176 yd [161 m]/50 g)

Lana Grossa
Ingolstädter Straße 86
85080 Gaimersheim, Germany
www.lanagrossa.de
Meilenweit Multi-Jacquard, fingering-weight sock (45% cotton, 42% wool, 13% polymide; 415 yd [380m]/100g)

Muench Yarns, Inc.
285 Bel Marin Keys Blvd., Unit J
Novato, CA 94949-5763
(415) 883-6375
www.muenchyarns.com
Touch Me, worsted-weight chenille (72% Rayon, 28% Wool; 61 yd [55 m]/50g)

Plymouth Yarn Company, Inc.
PO Box 28
Bristol, PA 19007
(215) 788-0459
plymouthyarn.com
Dazzlelash, eyelash novelty (78% polyester, 22% rayon; 220 yd [200 m]/50 g)
Encore, worsted-weight (75% Acrylic, 25% Wool; 200 yd [180 m]/100g)
Eros, ladder-type novelty (100% nylon, 165 yd [151 m]/50 g)
Firenze Bouclé, worsted-weight bouclé (30% wool, 30% acrylic, 40% nylon; 47 yd [51 m]/ 50g)
Sinsation, heavy worsted-weight chenille (80% rayon, 20% wool; 38 yd [35 m]/50 g)

Tahki • Stacy Charles, Inc.
8000 Cooper Ave. Building 1
Glendale, NY 11385
(800) 338-9276
www.tahkistacycharles.com
Cotton Classic, worsted-weight cotton, (100% mercerized cotton; 108 yd [99 m]/50 g)
Splash, ribbon-type novelty (75% Polymide, 25% Polyester; 114 yd [104 m]/50 g)

Trendsetter Yarns
16745 Saticoy #101
Van Nuys, CA 91406
Binario, ladder-type novelty (100% polyester; 82 yd [74 m]/25g)
Eyelash, eyelash novelty 100% polyester; 80 yd [72 m]/20 g)
Metal, eyelash novelty (100% polyester; 90 yd [81 m]/20 g)

Valley Fibers from Webs
Service Center Road
PO Box 147
Northampton, MA 01061-0147
(800) 367-9327
www.yarn.com
Brilloso, sportweight (64% rayon, 21% cotton, 15% acrylic; 1050 yd [960 m]/8 oz)
Heavy Rayon Chenille, heavy worsted-weight chenille (100% rayon; 474 yd [433 m]/ 16 oz)

YLI
161 West Main St.
Rock Hill, SC 29730
(803) 985-3100
ylicorp.com
Candlelight Metallic, metallic thread (100% metallic; 125 yd [114 m] spool)

Bibliography

Bertoglio-Giffin, Judith. *Bead Crochet Ropes.* Windham, New Hampshire: Glass Cat Designs, 2002.

Brown, Nancy. *The Crocheter's Companion.* Loveland, Colorado: Interweave Press, 2002.

Cosh, Sylvia, and James Walters. *The Crochet Workbook.* New York: St. Martin's Press, 1989.

Durant, Judith, and Jean Campbell. *The Beader's Companion.* Interweave Press: Loveland, Colorado, 1998.

Kliot, Jules and Kaethe, editors. *Bead Work, 2ⁿᵈ Edition.* Berkeley, California: Lacis Publications, 1984.

Kooler, Donna. *Encyclopedia of Crochet.* Little Rock, Arkansas: Leisure Arts Publications, 2002.

Perrenoud, Carol. *Bead Crochet Video Workshop.* Colfax, California: Victorian Video Productions, 1996.

Potter, Annie Louise. *A Living Mystery: the International Art & History of Crochet.* AJ Publishing International, 1990.

Schwartz, Lynell K. *Vintage Purses at Their Best.* Atglen, Pennsylvania: Schiffert Publishing, 1995.

Sommer, Elyse and Mike. *A New Look at Crochet.* New York: Crown Publishers, 1975.

Weldon and Company. *Victorian Crochet.* New York: Dover Publications, 1971 (a replication of *Weldon's Practical Crochet*) London, England c. 1895.

Weissman, Judith Reiter, and Wendy Lavitt. *Labors of Love—America's Textiles and Needlework, 1650–1930.* New York: Wings Books, a division of Random House, by arrangement of Alfred Knopf, 1987.

Wells, Carol Wilcox. *Creative Bead Weaving.* Asheville, North Carolina: Lark, 1998.

———. *The Art and Elegance of Bead Weaving.* Asheville, North Carolina: Sterling Books, 2002.

White, Mary. *How To Do Beadwork.* New York: Dover Publications, 1972.

Index